Marketing for Authors

Tonya Andrews
CEO/Owner
Crossroads Publishing, LLC

Marketing for Authors

Crossroads Publishing, LLC

620-204-1710

ISBN: 979-8-9926485-2-2

Author—Tonya Andrews

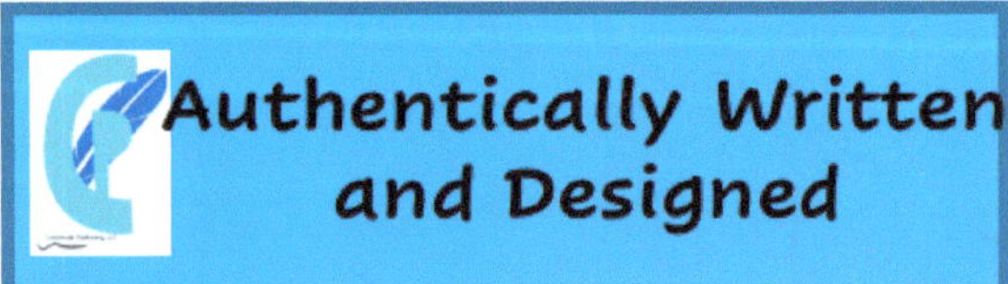

Table of Contents

Welcome to Marketing for Authors...

While marketing in general can seem like a very daunting task, please do not fret. It can and absolutely does become overwhelming at times, especially when you don't know where to start or how to accomplish it. There are so many options these days from social media, to newspaper hard copies, to magazines, to interview podcasts, to blogs and the list goes on and on. This book will help you navigate through, and hopefully provide tips and ideas for you to feel confident in marketing your own product. The main thing to remember as you learn this bit of marketing is that you can do it. It may take a few tries, and that is not a problem. It may take you a bit to understand how something works and that is how things go sometimes. It may take you reaching out for help, and believe me, that is ok! I am available to answer questions or give ideas. As an author myself, I totally understand the value of wanting to get your masterpiece out to the world. I understand the excitement of seeing it in print, and wanting to see it on a local bookstore shelf. I also understand the patience it takes to get it there. Marketing can be scary, and intimidating, however, the wisdom shared can also be a very beneficial asset to have as an author. Thank you for your interest in this book. Happy Marketing, friends!

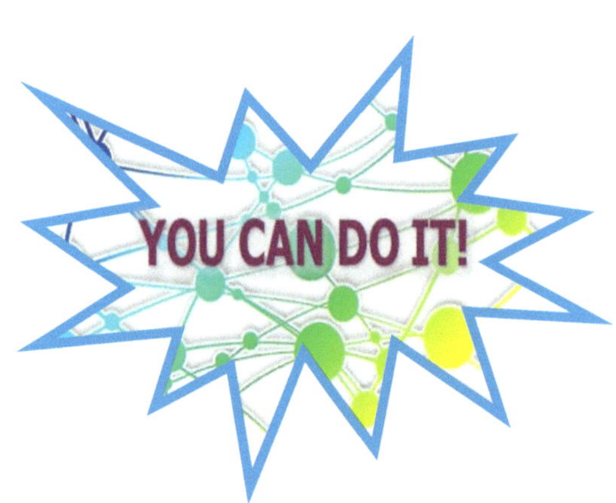

Introducing...

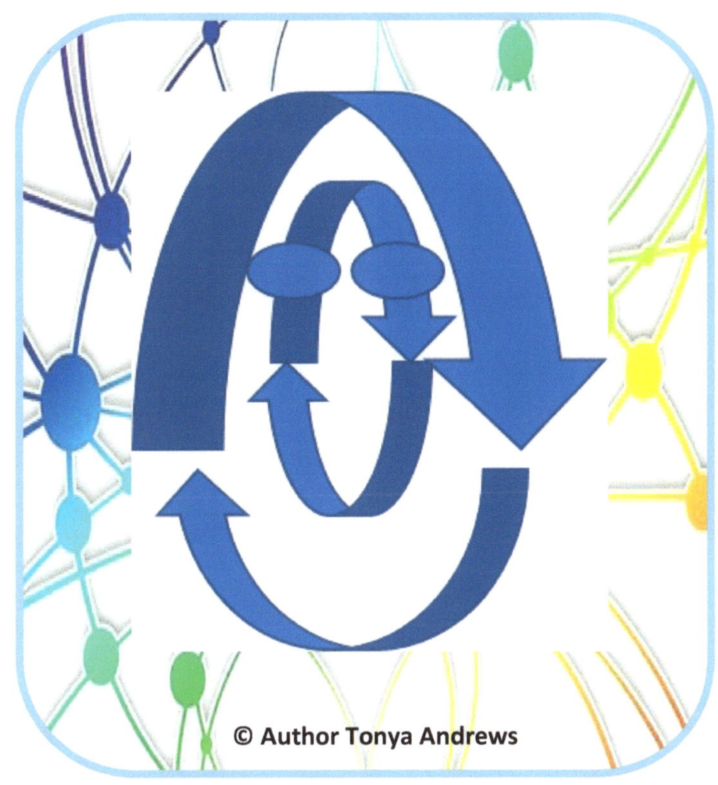

Marketing Mel

Marketing Mel will be seen throughout this book. There are many details and ideas that go into marketing. Marketing Mel will provide some of these along the way, and hopefully help you think differently and creatively. Marketing is a never ending cycle of learning and being creative.

Marketing by Book Phase

- ◊ Writing Phase
- ◊ Publishing Phase
- ◊ Book Release Phase

Marketing Ideas—Writing Phase

Whether you are still writing your book, in the publishing process or have the amazing finished copy in-hand, there are some marketing pointers to keep in mind. Marketing starts way before the published product hits the shelves. Here are a few ideas to consider as you write your masterpiece.

- First and foremost, decide what area your book will be classified as. If you are not sure, your publisher can help you with this. Will it be a children's book, a young adult's book, a cookbook, a coloring book, a devotional, non-fiction or another style? This will help you in moving forward in your marketing process.
- Stop in at local libraries and let them know you are working on writing a book. If it is a children's book, ask them if they have reading hours that you could maybe come for once published. If it is not a children's book, ask them what their process is for display. Also, inquire as to their process for acquiring local author books. Do they buy them? Do they have to be donated? Also, do they allow book signings and what is their process?
- Reach out to the local newspaper publication. Also let them know you are writing a book. They may want to do a story before the book is even published. A lot of times, it depends on what the story is about and if it compliments any current events. It does not hurt for them to have your contact information for possible mentions. It would be beneficial to ask for a contact email information to send them an author picture to use if wanted.
- Check-out your local bookstore options. Look around and see how they display, what their processes might be and also who you can contact about getting your books on the shelves once published. Also, what is their process for allowing book signings?

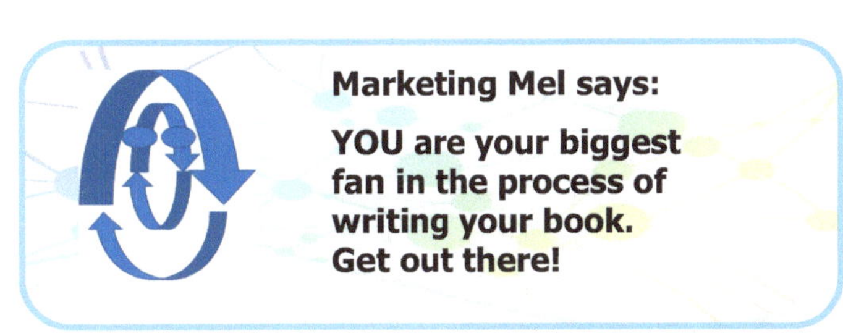

Marketing Ideas–Writing Phase

- ◊ Elementary schools are an excellent place to get your book noticed if you write children's books. While you are writing, a stop into the local elementary school office would be beneficial. See if they allow authors to visit and share their publications. Also, will they allow the author to provide an order form for kids to take home?
- ◊ Another idea for when you are writing your book would be to check into when there are local vender fairs of any sort. Sometimes, there is little to no cost to have a booth. This would require a pretty good sized purchase of books by the author well before the event, as well as looking into marketing materials to help sales.
- ◊ Finally, are there any writer's groups in your area? Do you have the knowledge and capability to start one if not? These sorts of groups can be very helpful and encouraging in many ways. Let's face it, writing is a challenge from the first word on through. If you are not sure if there is a writer's group in your area, that would be another inquiry for your local library.

As you can see, marketing is all about getting out there. Your book will not be known if you do not make an effort. Your publisher may indeed have a marketing department and offer some services. However, the marketing of your book is ultimately your responsibility, even with the time to learn and gain the wisdom of sharing it. You are the one that knows where the story came from, why and most importantly, the details that formed it. You are the best one to share your book. Be proud of it!

Marketing Ideas—Publishing Phase

Once your book goes into the being published phase, it is the time to get cracking on marketing your book. There are many options and ideas on how to get the information out there. Getting a digital copy of the cover from your publisher would be very beneficial in moving forward. Below are some ways to market your book before release.

◊ This is where the author website, author Facebook page and all social media comes into play. Websites can seem very daunting, and that is understandable. Crossroads Publishing, LLC offers website design for a decent fee. An author website and an author Facebook page can be very beneficial in a way to release information about your book in a concise, fast manner. They are very easy to create and set-up, and have amazing marketing value in that posts can be boosted and shared. These would do well to be created about a month before release date. Please note, some authors create this social media presence as soon as they start writing for blog options. However, in the interest of figuring out this marketing thing, one month before release date is sufficient.

◊ Another visit to the local newspaper would be helpful at this time. After discussions, you could email them the cover of your book so they can consider doing a date of release story. Some publishers do offer a press release option on your behalf, however, it would not hurt to make contact with the local publications as well.

◊ The local library may be interested to know the suggested date of your book. Most libraries are very happy to support local authors anyway they can. Inquire as to the process for displaying release date posters or if bookmarks with such information are allowed. Take a few moments to remind them that you would be available for book signing events, and if you have written a children's book, that you would be willing to read it during any children's times if needed. Depending on the topic of the book, you can ask them for book signing or reading times around the events in the book.

Marketing Ideas—Publishing Phase

- ◊ It would stand to reason that your local bookstores would definitely want to know your book is in the publishing process. Perhaps they would allow some release date posters as well, and be excited to learn of your story and when it will be available.

Marketing can be a very scary process, to be blatantly honest. However, it doesn't have to be when it is broken down into parts and pieces that can be accomplished step-by-step. You can do it!!

Notes:

Marketing Mel says:

An author website may be absolutely important in your writing career. Beyond that, the importance would be a Facebook Author Page, an Amazon Author Page and then the rest of the social media options.

Marketing Ideas–Book Release Phase

The day seemed like it would never come! It is finally here, the day your book is released to the world. Will it sell? Will people like it? Let me tell you, friends, this is the day you realize it was all worth it. There is just something about the day your book releases. Following are some marketing ideas for the joyous occasion.

- ◊ Talk it up big on your social media sites. This is where posts can be easily shared by friends and family, they can be boosted through Facebook for a minimal fee and the reach of social media is sometimes far beyond what we think.
- ◊ Visit your local libraries, coffee shops and bookstores to see if books signings are an option. The sooner you can start getting out there in the public with your book, the sooner it's amazingness will be known.
- ◊ If you have written a children's book, visit the local elementary school and ask if an author visit is now possible. Please don't forget to ask if an order form for the kids to take home is an option.
- ◊ Make contact and get information and prices on local vendor fairs. Now would be the time to sign-up for them and save your spot. However, make sure you have time to get books ordered.
- ◊ Share, share, share, share, share your book!! This is very important. People you know, people you are acquainted with, people you work with, share your book!

Marketing is really not all that daunting once it is looked at from a different perspective. Just take your time, and have fun! Yes, Marketing can be extremely fun.

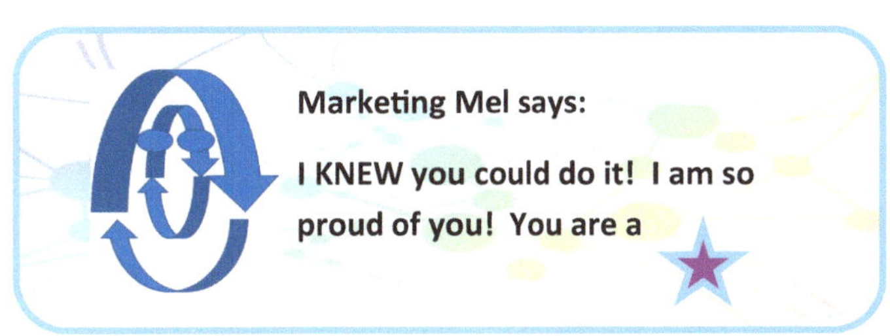

Marketing Ideas—Author Marketing Plan

Writing Phase:

- ◊ Decide what area your book will be classified as.
- ◊ Stop in at local libraries .
- ◊ Reach out to the local newspaper publication.
- ◊ Check-out your local bookstore options.
- ◊ Visit elementary schools.
- ◊ Research vendor fairs.
- ◊ Seek a local writer's group.

Publishing Phase:

- ◊ Social Media Creation.
- ◊ Revisit newspaper.
- ◊ Revisit library.
- ◊ Revisit bookstore.

Released Phase:

- ◊ Massive Social Media Campaign.
- ◊ Visit libraries, bookstores and coffee shops for book signing options.
- ◊ Visit the elementary schools for author visit options.
- ◊ Consider signing up for local vendor fairs.
- ◊ Share, share, share!
- ◊ Be happy! You did it! You are a published author!

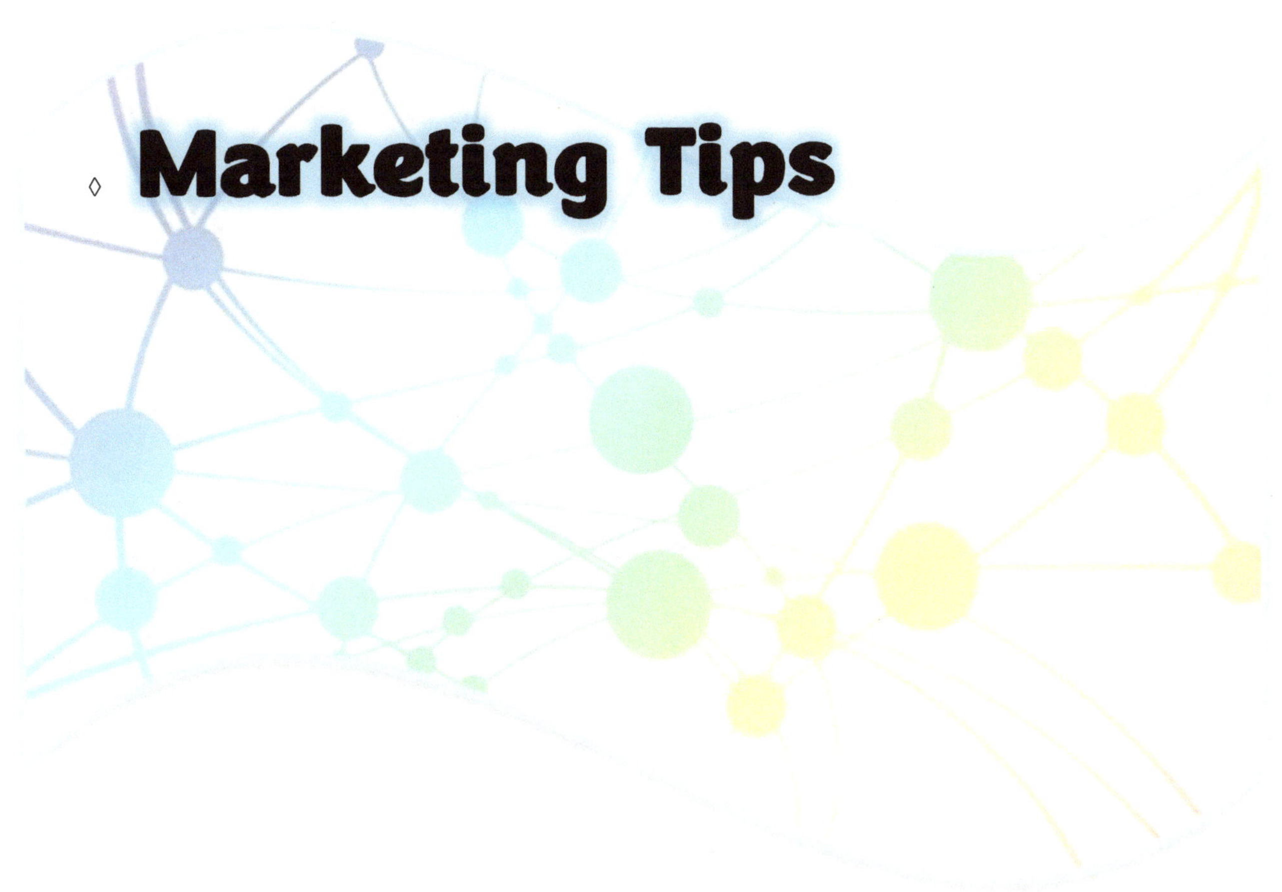

◊ Marketing Tips

Marketing Tips

One thing to keep in mind when working on any kind of Marketing piece, it is better if all of your items are formatted somewhat the same.

An easy way to do this is to create an Author Logo that will be used across the board in your marketing endeavors. A logo is created to catch eyes, for brand recognition so to say and to allow readers to recognize the author in any setting of information. They are sometimes easy to create and sometimes a challenge. If you need assistance, please contact me. I would be happy to assist you with some ideas. The logo can be used across the board on the Facebook page, website, posters, business cards, etc.

Along those same lines, it would be beneficial to use the same color scheme on each marketing piece or part of social media. This helps with the brand recognition.

Keeping fresh and new information and pictures uploaded and shared is another way to increase your reader following numbers. It will also encourage them to share more of your posts if you have new information frequently. This also pertains to new bookmarks and postcards at venues.

I have heard it said many times that less is more in marketing. I honestly think that this depends on the creator, what the goal of the item is and also what the person wants. There is a point to be made that sometimes marketing items can just have way too much information on them and people get lost trying to figure it out. However, with good design and colors, the right amount of information can always be displayed effectively.

If I have learned anything in marketing, it's that a lot of patience is needed. Not everything goes as it should, and it takes a lot of time to learn computer programs and the tricks to get them to do what you want with this or that picture or text. If you plan to do your own marketing creation, please consider some computer classes. Marketing is not an easy task if you don't have experience in it, however, anyone can learn it!

Just don't give up!

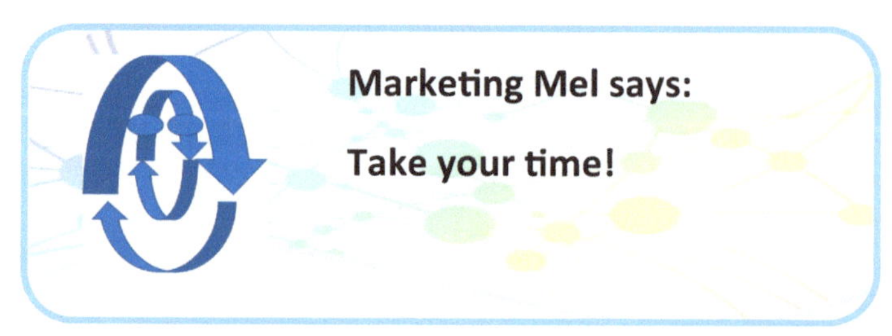

Marketing Tips

Patience, Patience, Patience

The age-old adage, Rome Wasn't Built in a Day, comes in very handy when it comes to marketing your writings. It takes a bit of time to first, get your name out there, and second, to consistently keep your products on the minds of buyers. There are so many products trying to grab consumers' attention these days. It just takes a patient, consistent reminder to those who may be interested in your writing for themselves or others.

Be Aware of your Surroundings

Does your local library have a winter or summer reading program? Perhaps you could read your books to the children there. If you have more adult level books, maybe the local library has a book club and your book can be included. Another option is an elementary school reading night, or even a presentation at a local college during a literacy event. There are many towns that have events with booths available. Do the local bookstores or libraries have a local author's signing events or could you (with help from Crossroads Publishing, LLC if needed) persuade them to start one? Also, another booth idea would be at local craft fairs or flea markets. There are so many options for getting your book out there. I would be happy to help you with any of them.

Smile, Smile, Smile

You are now a published author!! Be proud of that and SMILE! Sometimes, the best way to convey the writing in your book, is to share the story and background with a smile. That will allow the reader to fully understand the purpose of the book and where the idea and concept came from. It will also keep them engaged for more writings you may have published.

Share your Book

Do not be afraid to step out and share the information about your book in conversations, book stores, libraries, etc. A one-time donation of a book to a local library will help move things along nicely. Depending on the readership of that book, a reminder to the library about your writings at the next release(s) will be beneficial.

Jot it Down

Another part of Marketing is always keeping paper and pencil with you. Albeit, notebook and pen, journal and colored pencils, laptop, memo on phone, tablet or whatever is your preferred way to take notes. Many people may ask you many things, and it is very hard to keep track of it all at times. Also, you will see and hear so many ideas for more writings. Write it all down!! You will be very thankful you did later.

Use your Resources/Contacts

There is no shame or blame in asking family members or friends to help get the word out about your writings. It is a simple share of a post, or even just a mention in passing conversation. They are proud of you , and I'm sure, want to share all about your amazing writings.

Honestly, the most important Marketing Tip ever!!

Believe in yourself!! There will be many challenges, mountains, bumps, scrapes and fires along the way. You have gotten this far, and you cannot stop now. Keep moving forward, precept by precept. You can do it!!

Notes:

Marketing Tips

Top Hashtags: #amwriting; #writerslife; #romancewriter (your genre); #writerprompts; #author; #published; #writinganewbook; #comingsoon

Most authors spend 80% of their time marketing their book, but only 20% of their time preparing to market their book.

Take time to research and look at how other authors advertise their books and the posts they make. Take note of the ones that seem to have a lot of response.

It is the marketing that determines if your book will reach your readers or not.

You don't have to answer to anyone else as to why, how, who or what.

SAY THANK YOU!!

Ignore the haters.

Include the link to your book in every post after it's published.

Just because you wrote a book and got it published doesn't necessarily mean it will sell.

Be organized and prepared. Always have books and a signing pen with you, if possible. If not, keep a business card or postcard handy with the website where it can be found.

Make sure your readers know little specific details about your writing process such as writing, submitted to publisher, book contract signed, editing, illustrations being done, almost published, etc. It will keep them interested to want to know the next phase.

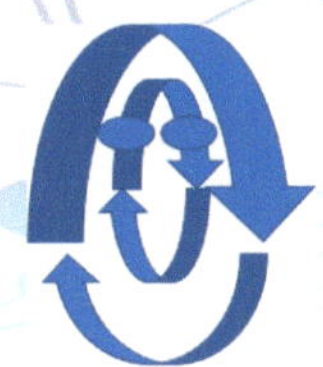

Marketing Mel says:

It is not as hard as it seems.

Selling Books

- Ways Books Can be Sold
- Royalties
- Pricing Books to Sell

Selling Books

Author Copies—These books can be designated by two different situations. The first one is when the Publisher sends the author a free copy of their just published book. It could also be the books that the author orders through the publisher. Both of these scenarios would qualify as author copies. This term could be used when selling, to bring more interest to the event or form. For example: There are only ten of these special order author copies available for this book signing event! They will be author signed! Get them before they are gone!

Purchasing Books—Some publishers allow authors to order books at a percent off amount. Please contact your publisher for their specific processes about ordering author copies. When you order author copies from the publisher at a percent off (plus tax and shipping) if they offer that option, you will not receive royalties on that purchase. Your money earned would be in how you price the books after receiving them. Books ordered straight from Amazon by the author are not considered author copies. However, ordering straight from Amazon would garner the normal royalty for purchasing of books from Amazon. If you are looking to make the most money on your book sales, your best bet would be ordering from the publisher at the provided percent off and selling them yourself or in one of the ways below. This not only allows you to sign the books before customers receive them, but also allows you the opportunity to build fellowships, answer questions if there might be any and set your own sale price for the book.

Ways Books Can Be Sold:

By Order Form—At any venue or around anyone you know, if you do not have books on-hand, a book order form can be filled out. You would be responsible for figuring the correct numbers. Sales tax needs to be added, and you can also add a shipping amount if you so choose. If you are doing a bigger order from order forms, the shipping cost could be less for each buyer. You would be responsible for getting the books ordered and shipped or delivered to the buyers. A Book Order Form is a very feasible option to consider for a school book reading event. The form would be emailed or provided to the school well in advance of the reading event. This would allow the forms to go home with the students and plenty of time for shipping, signing and organizing before the event. It would be good to have extra book order forms at the event as well in case all of the books are sold out. Crossroads Publishing, LLC provides this order form for author to use.

Amazon/Website/Online—This option is when customers are referred to any number of social media options to purchase the book. The author is not involved in the money exchange for this option. The book is ordered from that website online, they pay for shipping through that website and the book is shipped directly to them. The book could be signed at a later time by the author.

Ways Books Can be Sold at a Venue:

Author Provides—The author would provide all of the books and items needed to sell the books at an event. The author would set the price, figure tax in and also make sure that customers are satisfied with the purchase, etc. The venue receives no income from this option, unless the author would decide to offer a percentage. The best way to purchase books for this option is through the publisher at the percent off discount. Your money earned would be in the price you set the books to sell for.

Venue Provides: You would have to talk to your publisher to see if they offer this option. If a venue would like to purchase books for a signing event, they may purchase them from the publisher at a percent off discount. This amount can be discussed with the publisher. However, there are two very important parts of this. The venue must offer a percentage of sales to the author from the sale of the books ordered. Some publishers allow book returns if needed, and some do not. That would need to be discussed with the publisher and be in the contract. The percentage of sales must be worked out and agreed upon by the venue and the author. Crossroads Publishing, LLC can provide an agreement form for the author to use for this instance. With the venue ordering from the publisher, there would be no royalties involved with that sort of purchase. The other option is for the venue could also order the books outright from Amazon. The normal Amazon royalty to the author would apply in that case, and no agreement for percentage to the author would be needed. The venue would have to price the book considerably higher in this instance, banking on the signature of the author to be the difference in price.

Consignment: This means the author buys and provides the books on a consignment agreement. They are normally split 60/40 with the author receiving the higher amount. This option also allows the venue to keep the unsold books on shelves with a feasible option. Crossroads Publishing, LLC could provide an agreement form to be used for this instance as well.

Notes:

____

____

____

____

____

____

____

____

____

Royalties

Sometimes, in trying to figure a selling price for your book, royalties would need to be known. Below is a rough draft idea of how to figure out your royalties through Amazon KDP. Your publisher should also provide this information to you.

PAPERBACK EXAMPLE ONLY

Amazon—40% fee off the top of the list price to have the book on Amazon

Leaves 60% royalty from Amazon from the sale of the book at list price

- Minus Printing Costs (differs per book, your publisher will have this information when they upload the book into the publishing program)

-Minus Publisher percentage***

=

Equals Total Author Royalty

(paperback example only, any other type will have different numbers)

US Sales

$7.02—20% Publisher percentage***= $5.62 for each book sold royalty to the author

International Sales

$3.82—20% Publisher percentage*** = $3.06 for each book sold royalty to the author

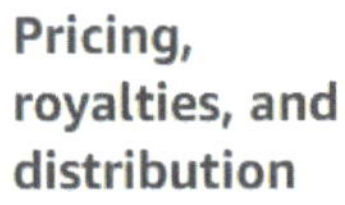

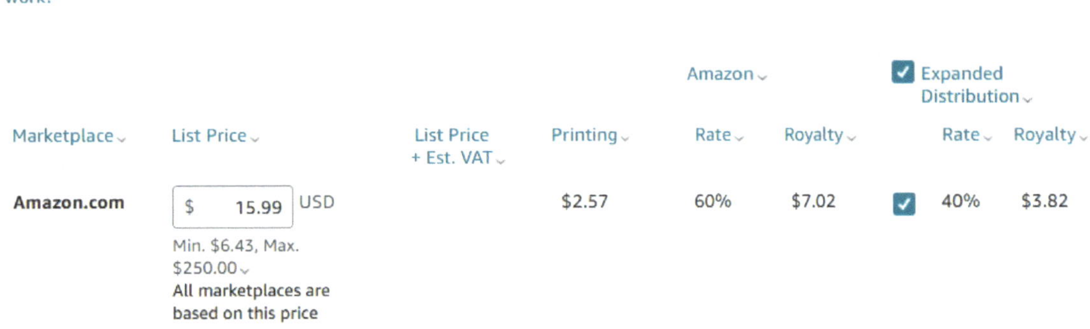

***_**EXAMPLE ONLY**_ (Publisher percentage will change based on what your publisher has deemed as their split and a signed book contract)

(screenshot from Amazon KDP showing actual royalties on a book)

Pricing Books for Vendor Events or Book Signing Events

The price of your book at vendor or book signing events depends solely on what you prefer. However, there are many things to consider.

The Price of the Book on Amazon—This is your starting point. Many authors think that they have to sell their books for this same amount, and that is untrue. The customers might notice if the book is priced higher at an event, however, many factors go into the price and can be explained.

The Venue—What kind of place where the book signing be held? A mall, a place with lots of shopping options or a tradeshow has many things to catch the eyes of customers. The price of the book definitely needs to be competitive, though still enough to make a profit.

The Genre—What genre is the book? Would it catch the attention of adults or children more? What experienced information is included in the book to consider in the price? Does it have phenomenal illustrations to up the price a bit?

The Time of Year—If the book signing event is in conjunction with anything holiday related, that could effect the price of the book as well. It could go either way with this. The author may want to price it a bit less in hopes of selling more. The marketing could be phrased as a holiday sale on the book. Another option would be to price it at a bit more, with the author signature or author copy wording.

Author Signature—If the book will have an author signature, it can be priced $10 to $20 higher than just the book itself. If the author is very popular and the book is predicted to be a best seller, that price added could be more depending on the preference of the author. If it would have the signature of who the book is dedicated to or about, the price could be increased by another $10 to $20 depending on the popularity of the person.

Sales Tax—Sales Tax must be added to the sale of most books. Please seek the information you need from your state to secure a Sales Tax Certificate or what they might term it. This means you will report information to the state usually quarterly about sales, etc. This makes your author journey a business and you will need to consider filing taxes with the federal government at the end of the year as well. Keep track of all of your income and expenses. If you need more assistance understanding this, please contact Tonya at Crossroads Publishing, LLC.

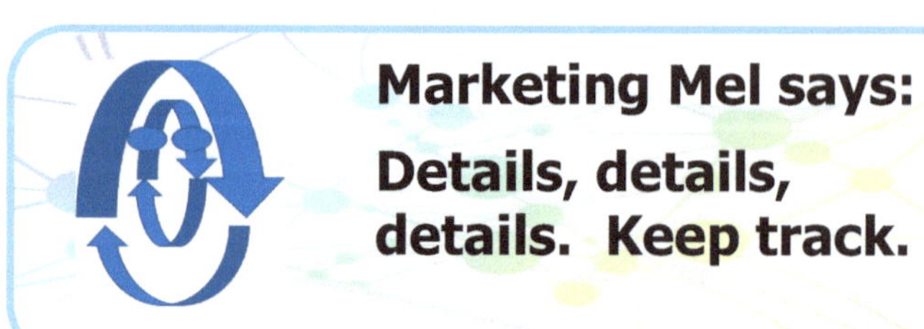

Pricing a Book Worksheet

List Price of the Book	____________
Author Signature Included	+____________
Dedication or Character Signature Included	+____________
Popularity of the Book/Series	+____________
Phenomenal Illustrations/Award Winning Illustrator	+____________
Experience on a Subject Included in the Book	+____________
Holiday Appeal	+____________
Venue/Event Appeal	+____________
Sales Tax	+____________
Total Per Book	____________

Marketing Materials

- Bookmarks
- Posters
- Business Cards
- Postcards

Marketing Materials

Sometimes, just as important as the books, are the marketing materials that you have to go along with them. There are many options, and not all of them cost a fortune.

- *Bookmarks*– These are very easy to create and print. If you have a word processing program on your computer, and a printer, you will be in business. If you do not have a printer, a local office products place would be an option.

- *Posters*– Posters can be very helpful before, during and after a book signing. Sometimes, venues will allow them to be posted to advertise an upcoming event. If you include contact information at the bottom, they can be a good reference source during a book signing.

- *Business Cards*– Business cards may seem a bit old-fashioned to some, however, they still serve their purpose. Depending on the crowd coming through, you may have quite a few that would be interested in business cards.

- *Postcards*— Postcards can be a handy option in listing books in a series, or letting readers know when upcoming books are set to be released.

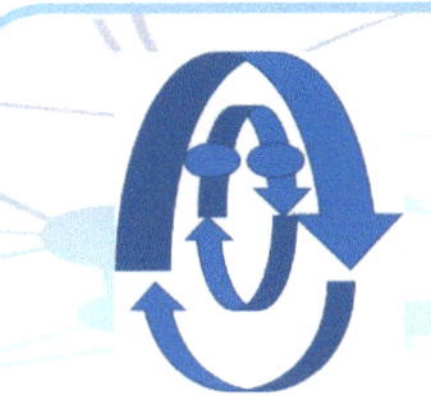

Marketing Mel says:

Not every single space has to be covered with information. I promise, some white space is acceptable.

Marketing Materials—Bookmarks

◊ *Bookmarks*– These are very easy to create and print. If you have a word processing program on your computer, and a printer, you will be in business. The process at home just takes a bit of time and patience in creating them, and also the lining up for printing. If you do not have a printer, a local office products place would be an option. Most generally, they will allow you to email the jpg of your bookmark creation to them and they will print them for you. A local office products store could also laminate them for you.

◊ Information to include on a bookmark:

Author Name

Book Title

Book Cover Picture

Short Description of Book

Facebook or Website for Author

Publisher Logo and Name

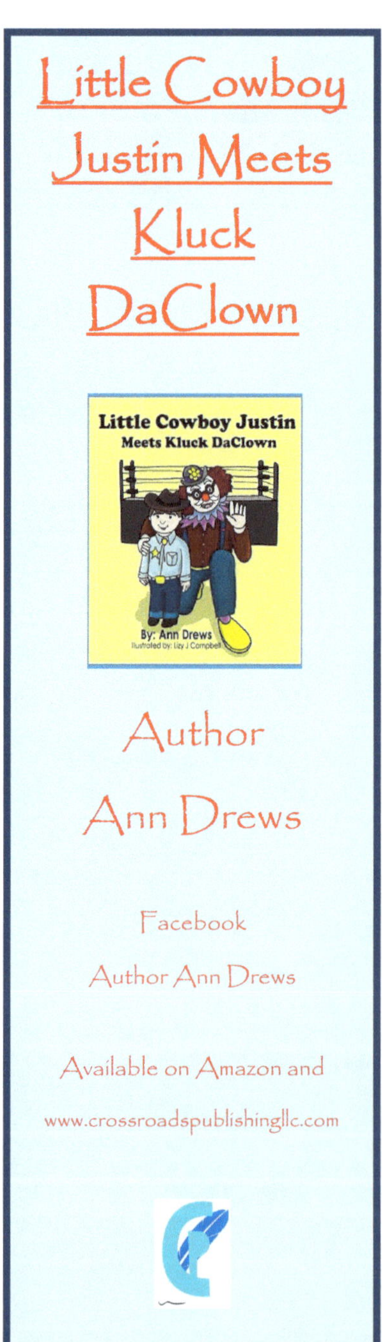

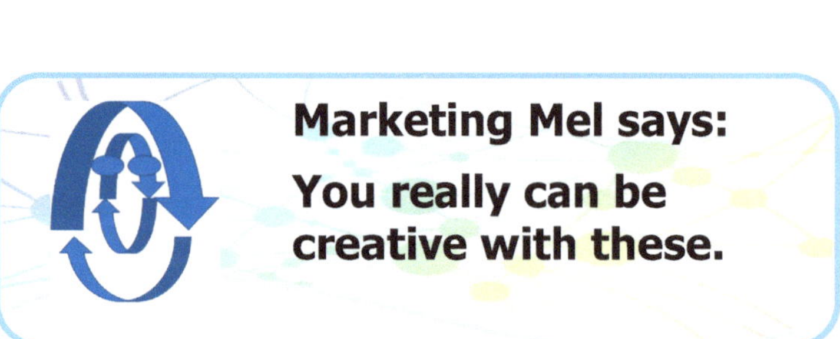

Marketing Materials–Posters

◊ *Posters–* Posters can be very helpful before, during and after a book signing. Sometimes, venues will allow them to be posted to advertise an upcoming event. If you include contact information at the bottom, they can be a good reference source during a book signing. As for after the event, if they do not include a specific date and time, they can be left up to create interest in your books. Another option would be to create one with event specific information and another without. The event specific poster could be removed, allowing the simple advertisement for the book to remain. An awesome option for creating posters is www.vistaprint.com. It is a very user friendly site, and cost effective.

◊ Information to include on a poster:

Author Name

Book Title

Book Cover Picture(s)

Short Description of Book(s)

Facebook or Website for Author

Publisher Logo and Name

Upcoming Book Signing Information

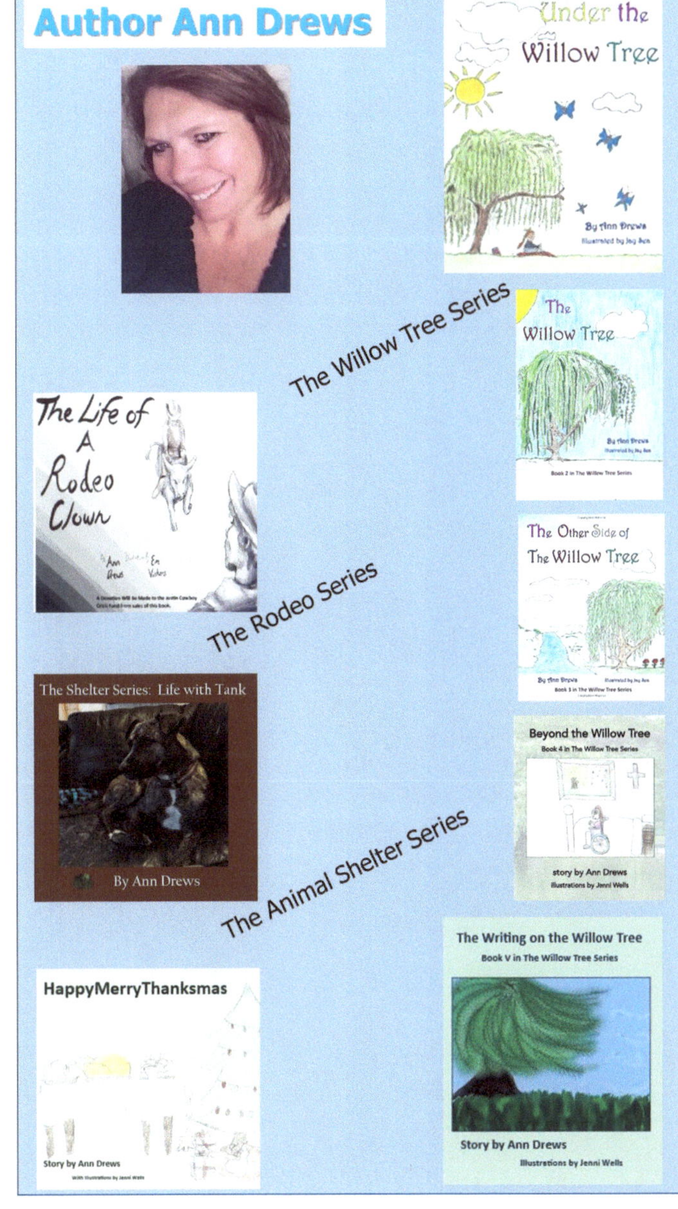

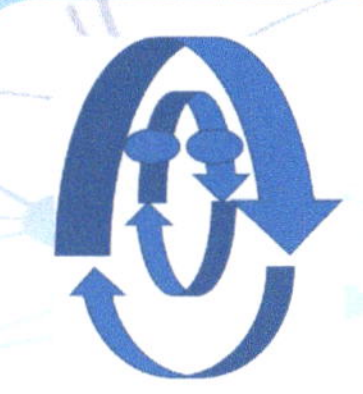

Marketing Mel says:

Inexpensive way to get out a lot of information.

Marketing Materials–Business Cards

◊ *Business Cards–* Business cards may seem a bit old-fashioned to some, however, they still serve their purpose. Depending on the crowd coming through, you may have quite a few that would be interested in business cards. They do not have to include much information, and they do not have to be fancy. Creation of these can be done at www.vistaprint.com as well. The cost effective option of printing with Vistaprint far outweighs creating them on your computer and printing them at home.

◊ Information to include on a business card:

Author Name

Book Title

Book Cover Picture

Facebook or Website for Author

Publisher Logo and Name (if it will fit)

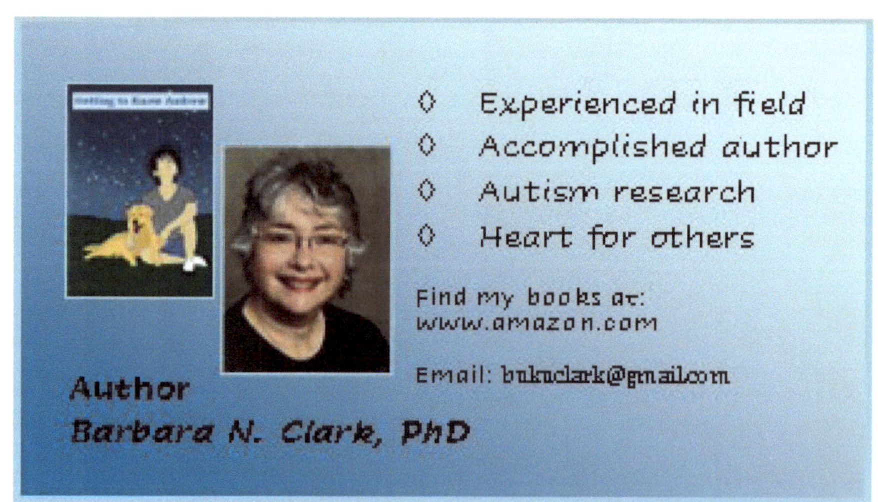

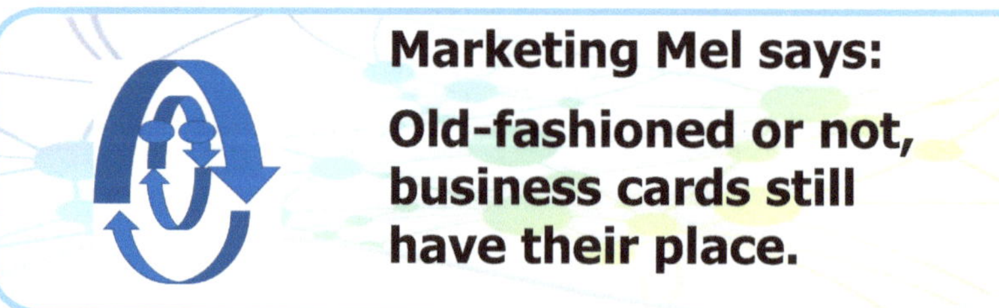

Marketing Materials–Sample Business Cards

Author Ann Drews

The Willow Tree Series

The Rodeo Series

The Animal Shelter Series

Facebook:

Author Ann Drews

Phone:

785-555-5555

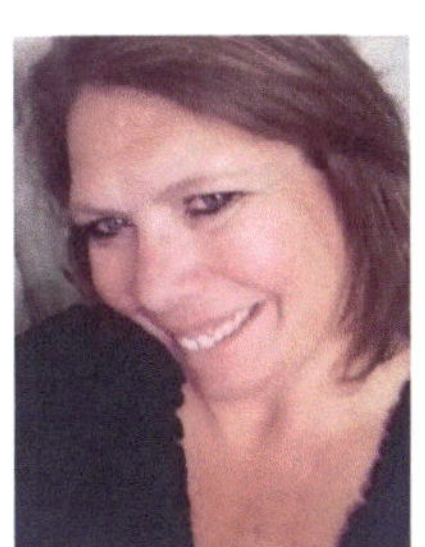

Facebook:

Author Ann Drews

Phone:

785-555-5555

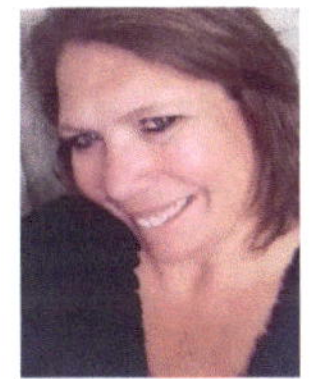

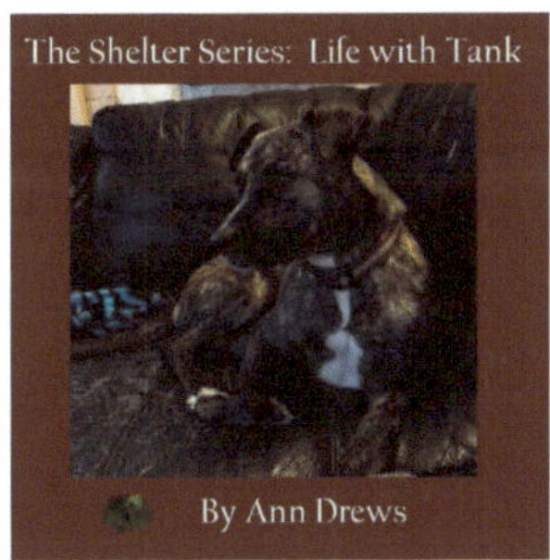

Author Ann Drews

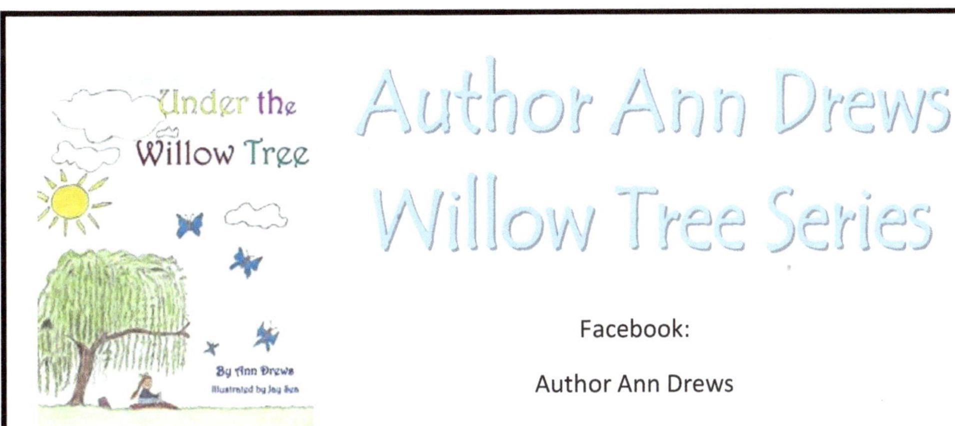

Marketing Materials–Postcards

- *Postcards*— Postcards can be a handy option in listing books in a series, or letting readers know when upcoming books are set to be released. It is basically just a simple informational piece to catch a reader's eye. It does not have to be full of information in the least. Sometimes, readers might pick them up to use as bookmarks. Sometimes they may put them on their fridge. In any case, it is an inexpensive way to get your book out there.

- Information to include on a postcard:

  Author Name

  Book Title

  Book Cover Picture

  Facebook or Website for Author

  Publisher Logo and Name

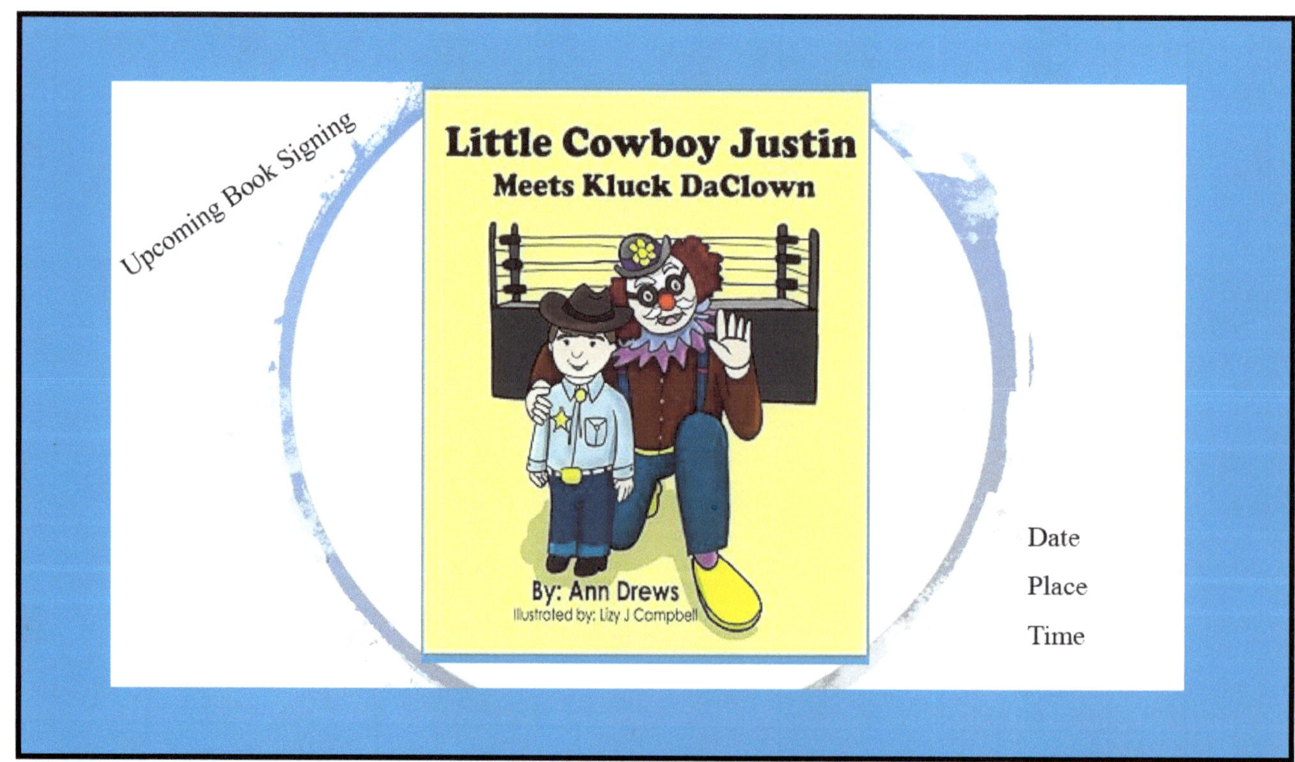

◊ Book Signing Event Tips

Book Signing Event Tips

Decisions, Decisions, Decisions – What theme do you want to go with for the table? Do you want to have a raffle for a free signed book? Do you need someone to assist you, and who would you invite to do that? Do you want to use regular black or blue pens, or get creative with colors and other options? Do you want to have other books you have written available for purchase and signature as well? Will you have bookmarks available?

Fellowship – One thing that can make a book signing go amazing is building fellowships. This can be with the owner or manager of the venue, those that work there, friends around you, family, co-workers, fellow church members, the list goes on and on. Building a good fellowship with those at the venue will allow options for repeat book signings. Fellowships with those around you allow for word of mouth information to pass and you to see more people attend your book signing.

Patience – I know, this is a challenging thought for many. Will my books get here? Will the marketing pieces be ready? Will the venue remember? Communication is the key, and helps tremendously with patience in these situations. Whether it is your first book signing, or your 50th, it can still be a bit unnerving. We are here to help you anyway we can including checking on things, providing updates, praying with you or even just simply listening. We are authors ourselves, and have a bit of understanding what you may be going through.

Organization – Going into a book signing unorganized only increases the wonder if it will go well or not. Having everything needed in line and in order to the best of your ability will not only help the event run smoother, but also, it will keep you balanced. You may consider a book signing tote to keep all needed items together. This will allow for organized storage as well as easy travel options.

Marketing – In casual conversation, with almost anyone, you can mention your book, what it is about and the book signing event. We don't always know how far our sphere of influence reaches.

Communication – As already mentioned, communication is indeed the key. It is so important, it needs its own bullet. Please, please do not feel like you are ever bothering anyone. Communicate with as many around you as possible about your book and upcoming events. Them passing on the information to others will help your volume of traffic on the big day.

Author Sales Tax Certificate—This is to be filed with your local state and needs to be secured before you have a book signing event if you are selling books. If you have an accountant, they can help you figure out the steps to get one. In most states, tax has to be charged when you are selling books at an event, at home or anywhere. Also, please consider there may be quarterly or yearly reports to file with the state and taxes paid on books sold.

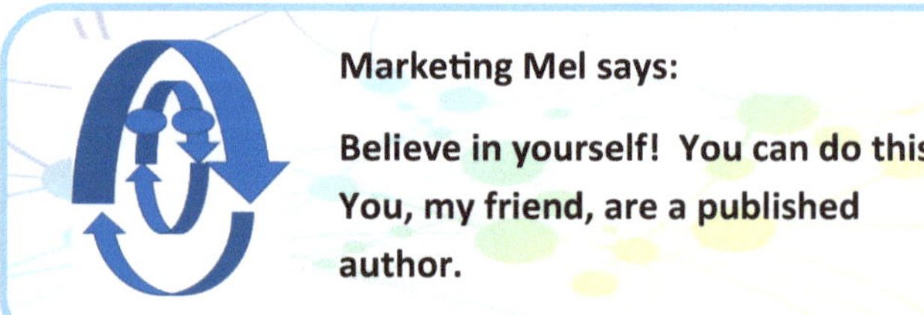

Book Signing Event Timeline

Make note of when your book signing is scheduled, where and the time.

____

4 weeks before book signing event –

- Order books needed.
  Date ordered________ Number ordered______
- Order marketing materials needed.
  Package ordered________ Date ordered___________

3 weeks before book signing event –

- Visit venue, make contact, ask if poster/fliers can be placed for advertising.
- Check on books ordered.
  Note arrival date.____________________
- Check on Marketing materials ordered.
  Note arrival date.__________

2 weeks before book signing event –

- Gather needed items.
  - Table (if needed, you may consider buying one, they are sometimes provided).
  - Tablecloth (author related, holiday related, region related, solid color).
  - Several working pens.
  - Monetary change if selling books at event.
  - Money bag of sorts.
  - Way of accepting debit card payment if going that route.
  - Thank you card for venue.
  - Basket for raffle drawing of signed book if doing one.
  - Raffle drawing slips of paper if needed.
  - Books to be sold and signed.
  - Bookmarks.
  - Posters.
  - Fliers of prior and upcoming releases.
  - Business Cards.
  - Books!

1 week before book signing event –

- Make contact with venue to remind/verify

Day of event

- Breathe!!
- Have fun!!
- SMILE! You are amazing!

Book Signings—Sample Email for Venue

Please find below an example of an email you can send to local coffee shops, libraries, book stores and schools. While your publisher may be doing this as well, it does not hurt to have multiple contacts going to the venues.

Simple Email

To: Contact at local library, local coffee shop or local bookstore

From: the amazing you

I am contacting you in regard to my book that was recently published. It is titled, "My Amazing Book Title Here", and it was released by (Your Publisher Name Here) on (Date Published).

This is the Amazon link to my book. (insert link here)

I would be interested in the possibility of a book signing at your venue or business if they are allowed. There are a few options for the availability of the books for the event that can be discussed.

Can you please let me know the process for author book signings?

Thank you in advance.

Your Name

Book Signings—Your Display

Display Options:

- *Decorative Tablecloth*—This can be holiday themed, a nice pattern or even just a solid color. No matter which you choose, it can dress up the presentation a bit. If you choose to do a lot of holiday decorations, a plain tablecloth would probably be a better option.
- *Holiday Decorations*—Decorating your table for an upcoming holiday can be fun for everyone involved. Going overboard would not be suggested, but perhaps some lights along the front of the table and a few table displays would be noticeable. The candy bowl and drawing basket could also be holiday themed.
- *Book Holders*—There are many options to be had to display your books. Your books can be put nicely on the table, however, they are better seen in a display of some kind. Choose what is best for your style and the area you will have to set-up.

www.displays2go.com

$41.99 $65.99

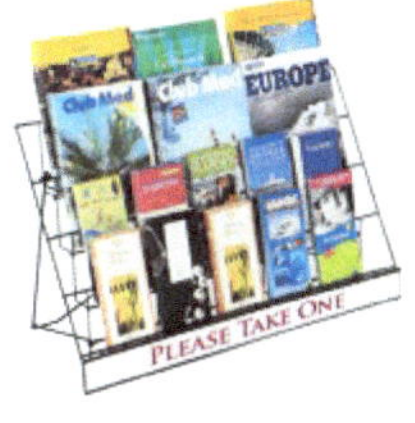

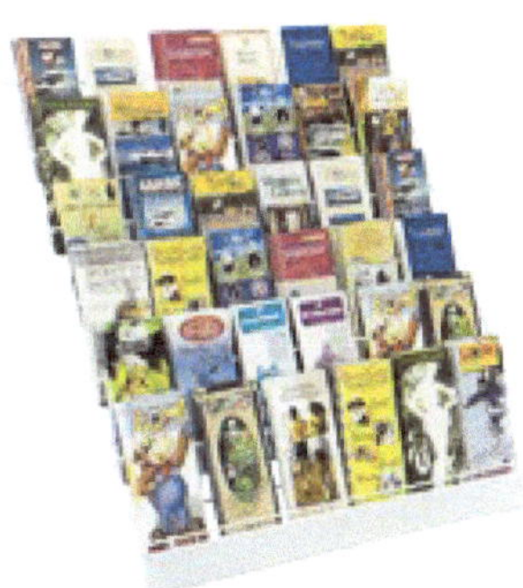

www.amazon.com

$14.99 $9.99

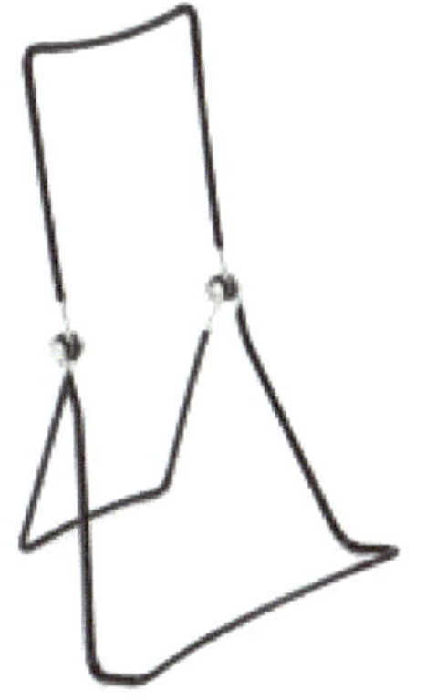

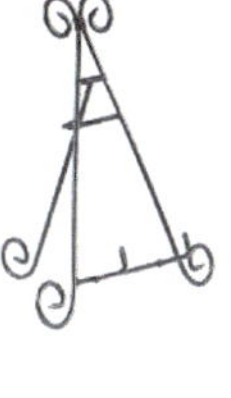

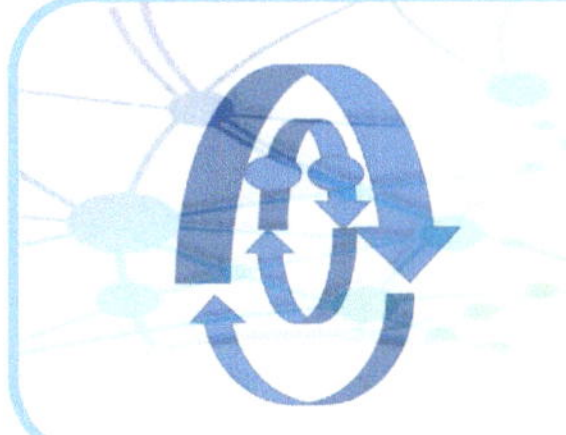

Marketing Mel says:

Checklist 1... 2... and 3!! You might remember all you need that way!

Book Signings—Your Display

- *Marketing Materials*—Sometimes, just as important as the books, are the marketing materials that you have to go along with them. There are many options, and not all of them cost a fortune. There is a section in this workbook about Marketing Materials. Bookmarks, postcards, business cards, posters and brochures are all amazing options for book signing events.
- *Books, Books, Books*—Make sure to order your books plenty in advance of the book signing event. If you are doing the event for one book, you will need about 20 to 30 books. This would be a larger amount if it is a larger event. There is no problem having 3 to 5 copies of your other books available.
- *Pens, Notepads* — Pens and paper to write on always come in very handy at a book signing event. You never know who wants to write down information, or what you may need to make note of. Having them printed with your author information is a consideration.
- *Drawing, Raffle*—Another option for a book signing is to have a drawing for a free book or a raffle. You would need the slips of paper, pens and a basket to put the slips of paper in. There are many options for the basket. It can be plain, or can even be holiday related. Make sure there is information displayed about when the drawing will be and how the winner will be contacted. It also needs to note if they need to be present to win.
- *Candy Bowl*—Some authors like to have a candy bowl on their tables. This can be a pro or a con to the table depending on the event and how the day goes. If there will be a lot of children attending, maybe a better option would be a few gift bags with a bookmark in it. There are hazards such as children choking if it is a free and open bowl of candy.
- *Shopping Bags*—A minor option that can be included would be some short of shopping bag. There are options for printed shopping bags as well. This could be another way to get your book out there, however, this could prove to cost quite a bit more than other options.
- Many of these extras and ideas can be created and printed through www.vistaprint.com. If you would need help with any of these ideas or how to order them, contact Tonya at ceo@crossroadspublishingllc.com.

Book Signings—Display Example

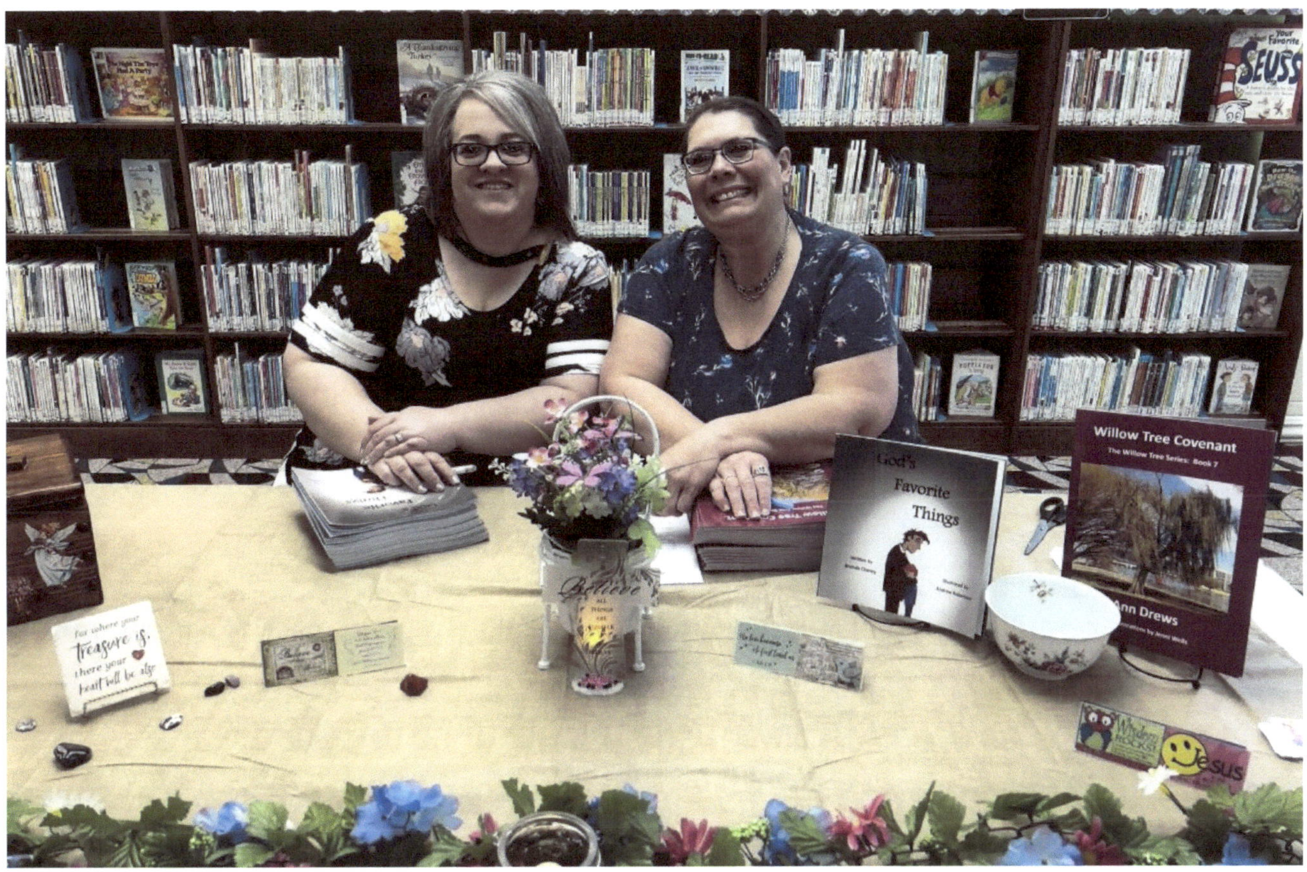

Author Brenda Cheney and Author Tonya Andrews ready for their book signing event at a local library.

Thank you to the library that allowed us to have this book signing event. They were very helpful in advertising it, and also showing people where to go in the library to find us, etc. They had the table ready for us, and also were very encouraging and supportive.

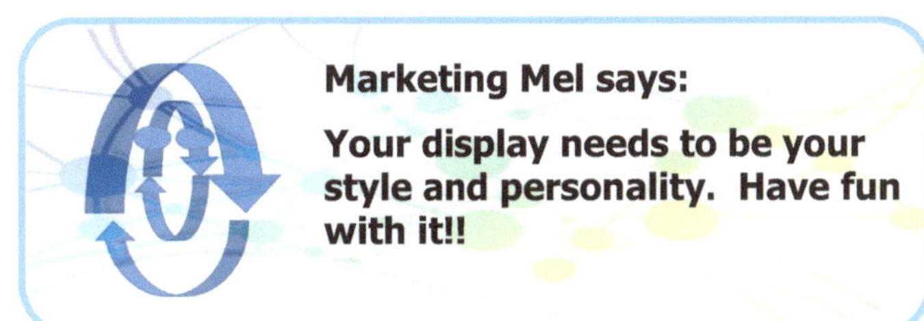

Book Signings—Reading Your Book

- First and foremost, smile, smile, smile! :D Be happy you are an author and you are able to share it with an audience.
- If there is only one person, read your book to them anyway. You never know what that one person might need out of your presentation.
- Sit somewhere towards the front of the area, but not necessarily front and center. If you sit a bit to the side, more people can maneuver to see you. Also, depending on the set-up, maybe standing would be a better option.
- Make sure to thank the venue as many times as you can during the reading. Most usually there is not a charge, so it is simply free advertising for you
- Always give a quick background of you but most importantly, how you became an author. Why, how, when, the steps or path that lead to it can all be very interesting to those listening. It may encourage them to do the same.
- For a children's book, the entire book can certainly be read. For a chapter book or novel, pick a few places where it tells part of the story and will intrigue the readers to want to get the book.
- Make sure to hold your book up high enough that everyone can see. Hold it away from you as to give plenty of space to turn pages.
- Give them time to see the pictures and words on the pages as you read. I always wait a few moments before turning the pages.
- Read the words slow, but animated. Tell your story!! Who better to bring your book to life than the one that poured heart and soul into writing it. Before I became an author, I was an Assistant Librarian in two elementary schools. My favorite days were the ones I was allowed to read to the kids. Do not let anyone tell you it is too much, or over the top or you are too obnoxious.
- Allow and offer a time for questions after the reading. You will be surprised what thoughts your book bring about, in children and adults.
- Also allow time for the audience to look at your book.
- Thank them for coming!
- Thank them for listening!
- Make your book available for purchase and signature.

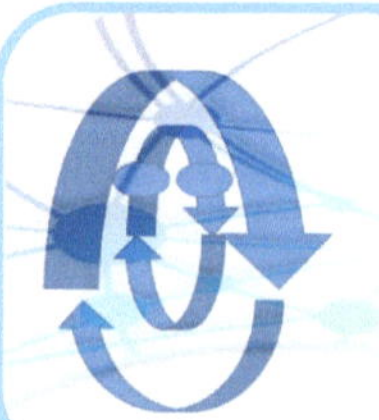

"If you fill your face with laughing, there will be no more room for crying." ~Rohinton Mistry, A Fine Balance

Sample Books Sales–Orders Tracking Spreadsheet

By using a simple expenses and profit spreadsheet you can keep track of your profit and loss. It doesn't have to be complicated and you don't necessarily need an accountant, but you must keep track of these things for possible tax purposes. Not only should you keep track of books purchases and sales, but keep track of expenses.

In the example below, the author bought five books from their publisher to sell at the costs outlined below. It is important to keep track of shipping and tax separately. Then the bottom section shows how many books of those five the author sold, leaving a profit of $62.02.

We also suggest starting a separate checking account for your book sales/purchases to make it easier to keep track of. Any expenses associated with marketing, sales, events, etc. should come out of this account.

Book Sales/Ordering Tracking Spreadsheet

Book Title

	Date of Order	Qty Bought	Unit Cost	Shipping per book	Tax per book	Subtotal
Books Ordered (Expense)	5/15/2019	5	$5.49	$2.00	$0.38	**39.35**
				Subtotal		**39.35**
	Date of Sale	**Qty Sold**	**Unit Price**	**Shipping Charged**	**Tax Charged**	**Total Sale**
Book Sales (Income)	6/1/2019	1	$15.99	$2.38	$1.12	**19.49**
	6/2/2019	4	$15.99	$0.00	$4.48	**81.88**
				Subtotal		**101.37**
				Profit / Loss		**62.02**

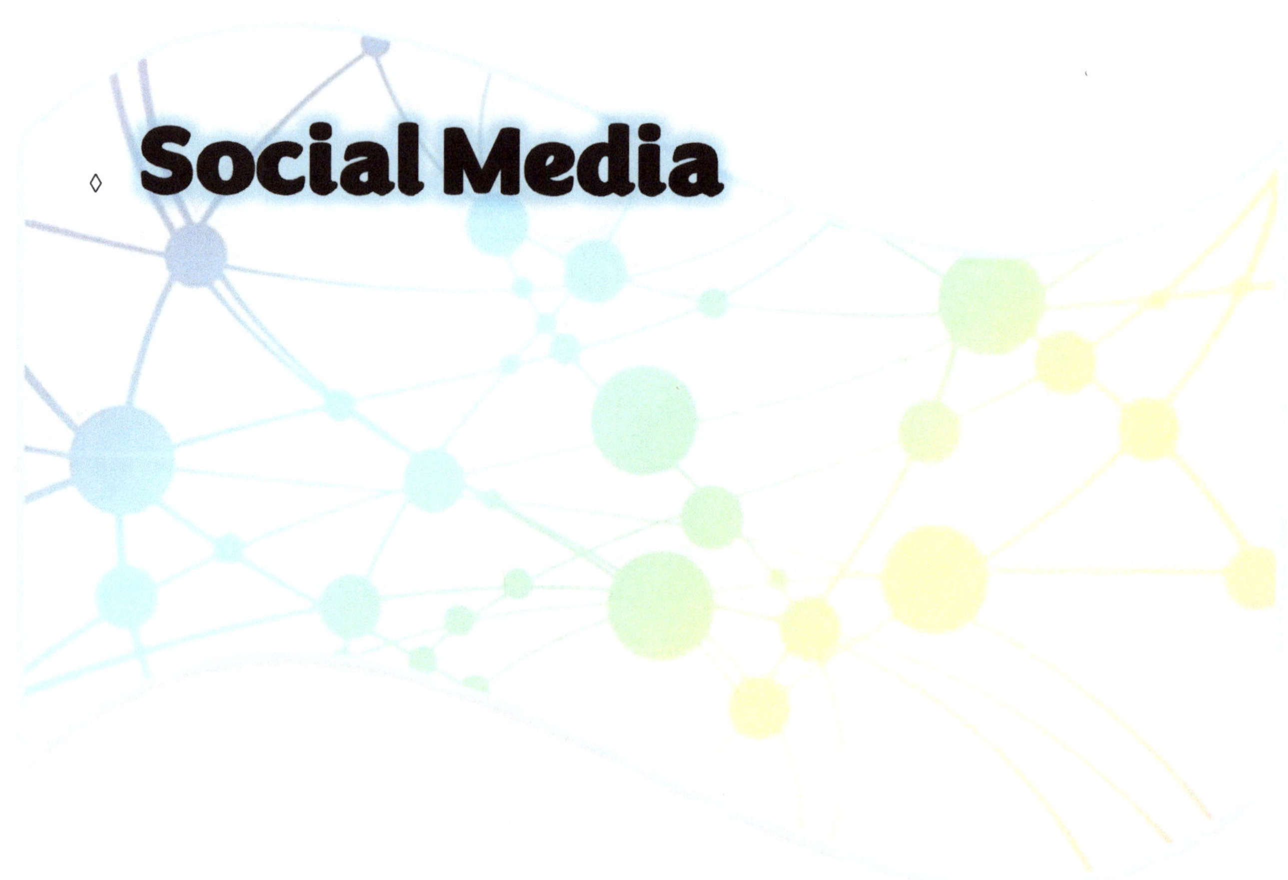

◊ Social Media

Social Media Information

- ◊ Almost 90% of marketers say their social marketing efforts have increased exposure for their business, and 75% say they've increased traffic. More than 50% of marketers who have been implementing social media marketing tactics for two years have reported improved sales.

  (www.smallbiztrends.com)

- ◊ Some social media disadvantages include real-time customer complaints and possible feedback. Your business is completely open to the public for scrutiny. It also means an increased use of business and personal resources to manage and control your social media. With modern technology today, people are theoretically constantly available. This can create descent when customers may think you should answer a message or email right away, whether it be your day to relax or you are dealing with something. Setting clear guidelines about this in the beginning helps alleviate these challenges. A simple message on your website or Facebook page letting them know that you may not answer communication right away would suffice.

- ◊ One major advantage to social media is the largely cost effective way of advertising. Facebook posts are free, and for a minimal fee, you can boost those posts. Creating a website certainly has domain and hosting costs included, however, updating as many times as you want has no cost. Twitter and Instagram are all free apps and ways to get information out about your books. There are also many groups on Facebook that will allow you to post updates and book information.

- ◊ There are risks involved. Identify theft, fake requests, social sharing risks, profile hacking and malicious links are just a few. If you step into the social media realm, it would be beneficial to have a very good anti-virus program on your computer and phone. There are a few free ones such as AVG, and there are also those that cost a decent fee. The ones that cost usually do a much better job protecting your electronics.

- ◊ The more places you are on Social Media the better you get your name/book out there. Set up a Twitter account, an Instagram Account, LinkedIn, etc.

Social Media Information

◊ Social media marketing has become an inevitable part of online marketing for companies and brands today. Your media planning requires a strong social media strategy that can amplify and expand the presence of your business in the digital world.

(www.amplispot.com)

◊ 10 Things You Must Do to Grow Your Online Business

1. Carefully target the online audience.
2. Create high-quality content and deliver it at high speed.
3. Personalize content.
4. Invest in mobile capabilities.
5. Integrate sales channels.
6. Consider subscription.
7. Remember logistics.
8. Skip the middlemen.

(www.entrepreneur.com)

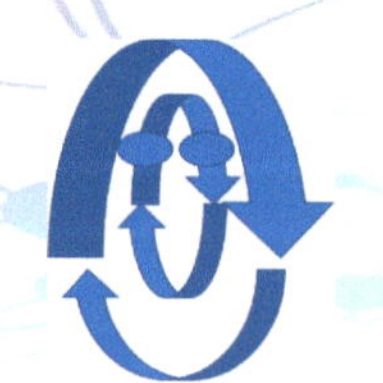

Marketing Mel says:

Being an author is a business. Keep track of income and expenses, and all needed things for taxes.

Social Media Calendar

Daily

- ◊ Reply to any messages you receive in messenger or on your page.
- ◊ Monitor posts that you are tagged in and respond as needed.
- ◊ Check current trending topics for language to include and avoid.
- ◊ Schedule posts according ahead so that they post even if you are busy.
- ◊ Update posts for special promotions for your book.
- ◊ Post from your blogs, videos, podcasts, etc.
- ◊ Monitor other author's posts for ideas, responses, trends.
- ◊ Engage with active followers and fans.

Weekly

- ◊ Connect with new authors on social media platforms.
- ◊ Check analytics and adjust scheduling and topics as needed.
- ◊ Create and monitor weekly goals for engagement, consistency, growth.
- ◊ Strategize with your publisher and post about upcoming events.
- ◊ Check analytics for paid ads and adjust as needed.

Monthly

- ◊ Check analytics for all platforms and consider needed adjustments to scheduling, topics.
- ◊ Research and try a new strategy each month; flag for follow-up analytics.
- ◊ Set goals and reminders for the next month.
- ◊ Offer to be interviewed on other's blogs and post a link to those that have interviewed you.

Quarterly

- ◊ Review analytics quarterly and consider needed adjustment to scheduling, topics.
- ◊ Consider strategy changes for paid and organic audiences.
- ◊ Review new strategies—integrate winning attempts and discard those that didn't get results.
- ◊ Weigh what posts worked ("likes) and what didn't and focus on those successful posts.

Annually

- ◊ Review what worked and what did not over the previous year.
- ◊ Consider brand messaging and adjust as needed.
- ◊ Work with your publisher to set up events for the upcoming year.

Author Website

There are many steps and process to creating an author website. It can be done by the author, however, it takes a lot of patience. If you can find someone to create one for you, that is the better way to go. It is very time consuming and can be very frustrating if you do not have the knowledge. Please see below for some basic instructions and ideas when it comes to an author website.

1. First of all, you will need to decide what site you wish to use for your website. Www.godaddy.com and www.wix.com are very nice options. Look into both and decide which one you would like to go with.
2. Securing a domain name would be next. The domain name is what is put into a browser to find your site. We suggest www.authorfirstnamelastname.com. This allows many books and publications, blogs and pictures and ideas to be added to the site and not be specific to just one publication.
   Example: www.authortonyaandrews.com
3. Whatever site you secure a domain with will allow you to create a simple one page website from there. They both have toolboxes and bars that allow you to easily click and add what you need to. There will be a monthly fee involved with the hosting of the website. This charge is different from the domain. The monthly fee will allow you to keep your website up and running, so that there will be something for people to see when they click on your domain. Paying the monthly fee will allow you to have multiple pages on your website if you wish.
4. The top or first page of your website should include your author name and perhaps a picture of you. It should be fairly simple and also then include a brief introduction of who you are and maybe why you are an author.
5. Your first page should also have a "Contact Me" box so that a reader can send you an email, review, or ask a question.

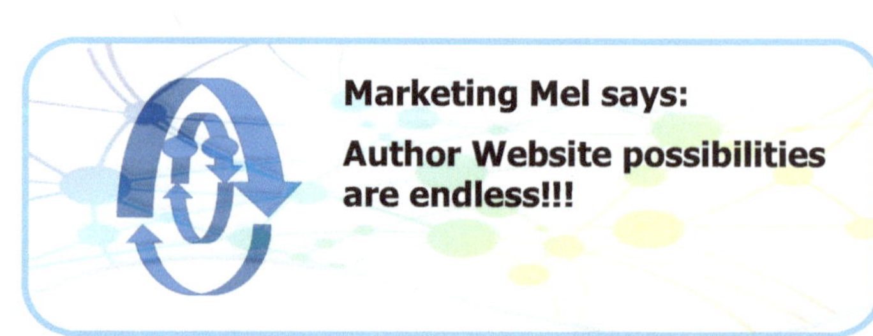

6. The next page can be an about you page. It can include your history, your trials and challenges, your good experiences as an author and also some pictures.
7. A bookstore could be included on the next page of your author website. There are many online options for paying. Both of the sites listed allow an easy option for adding a bookstore and information needed. If you don't choose to allow readers to buy directly from your website, then consider adding links to either your book on Amazon or on your publisher's website. If you have a bookstore on your website, this means you will need to have your books in stock and available to mail to the customers when they order from your website. The website will charge them tax and shipping if you choose to go this route.
8. Another page on your website could include pictures and information on all of your books. This will allow people to see what you have written and what is coming next. Include links to where the books can be purchased.
9. A blog would be an amazing way to get your thoughts out there as a writer. You can share your writing process, your thoughts, your challenges, what you have found that works or does not, etc. In between publishing, a blog is an easy way to keep readers returning to your webpage to not only read the blog, but also see your books and the progress on them.
10. A final page on your website can be events. You can let your readers know when books signings are coming up and also provide pictures of past events.
11. An optional page on your author website would be what other events or hobbies you are involved in. This is a good way for readers to get to know the author, and maybe become more interested in their books.
12. Make sure your website is mobile-friendly so readers can view it on their phone or table. The website hosts allow views of the website for laptop and mobile before publishing the page.

Crossroads Publishing, LLC offers assistance with setting up a website for a minimal fee. Please contact them at www.crossroadspublishingllc.com for more information

"A website is a window through which your business says hello to the world.

- Amit Kalantri

Author Biography Example

An Author Biography is very important for the publisher's webpage information, for press releases and also sometimes on your books. It needs to be fairly short, but also detailed. It needs to draw readers in. It needs to tell about you, and most importantly, why you are an author or how you became one.

Author Ann Drews was born and raise in Central Kansas. She has been writing poems since a very young age and was thrilled when God lead her to start writing children's books. It was a nerve wracking process to get her first book published, and even with her first publisher closing their doors, she persevered in the strength of Christ. She has many children's books now published with Crossroads Publishing, LLC and is working on quite a few more. Drews is surrounded by many who love and support her writing. She is very blessed to be allowed to share her stories with readers.

Be sure to include your picture with your biography on your book and to your publisher for their website.

Notes or Rough Draft Biography:

____

____

____

____

____

____

____

____

____

____

____

____

____

____

____

____

____

Social Media Posting

◊ What do we share?

1. As little as possible in regard to personal information.

2. Much can be misconstrued or mistaken. Short, sweet, to the point communications.

3. One main form of contacting you. Stick with one way, and if they post they want to communicate with you, encourage them to contact you in that one way. Do not engage in lengthy conversations on social media.

4. Book cover, book blurb, link to Amazon, awards won. Be mindful of timing in the publishing process, and what can be stolen for the benefit of others. As a suggestion, do not post or share book covers, words from the book or anything that can be taken from you until the book is published. It is just an added safety and protection for your hard work.

5. Referrals from others are an excellent thing to share on social media.

6. Be creative with your posts.

7. Always include the link to your book with every post.

◊ How often do we share?

1. Everyday is a bit much.

2. Every other day might be a bit much on every social media platform.

3. Every few days something small to keep interest.

4. Once a week, larger update post.

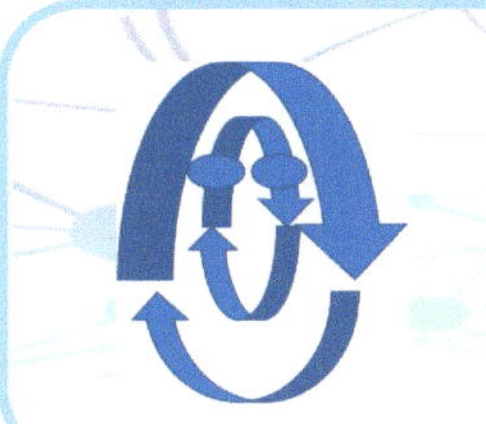

Marketing Mel says:

It takes time to figure out what kind of posts work on each social media platform. Experiment and see what you get the most response with.

Social Media Posting

◊ Where do we share our author and book information?

1. Places you know how to post or can figure out.
2. Facebook, Instagram, X, TikTok, Youtube.
3. Apps that will have the best benefit for your target audience.
4. Apps that you know a unique way of posting to get attention, such a polls, referrals, raffles for books, etc.

◊ Don't play the drama game!

1. Some post just to get an argument.
2. Some post just to be judgmental.
3. Some post because they are jealous.
4. Some post to take your information/ideas.
5. Some post just to be rude.

Steps you can take— Ignore, Delete, Block

Marketing Mel says:

You do not have to explain anything to anyone. Being an author is your gift, and your business. You do not have to play the drama game to be successful.

Social Media Posting Examples

Submitted Book-

Hello faithful book readers! I have some wonderful news to share with you. I have submitted my book to Crossroads Publishing, LLC. I am so excited to get this book going and published. Keep checking back for more. I will keep you updated. Thank you for walking this journey with me.

Book Contract Signed-

Good News! Good News! I have just submitted the signed book contract to Crossroads Publishing, LLC! This has already been an amazing journey so far. The next part of the process is editing. It would then be on to illustrations. The process to a published book as begun. Thank you for believing in me.

Book Completed Editing or Illustrations or Both-

What a great day! My book has made it through the editing process at Crossroads Publishing, LLC. It now moves on to the layout and format phase. This is where the publisher gets it read for upload to be published. This can be an interesting process, though all necessary. We are getting closer! I can't wait to share my book with you all. Thank you for your kind comments and support.

Author Zoom to see Book-

Let me just tell you, faithful readers, I just saw my book in layout and format with Crossroads Publishing, LLC, and it's going to be so wonderful! The next step is for the publisher to order the hard copy book proof. They will mail that to me to look over as well. Thank you for taking the time to read my posts and comment.

Book Proof Complete-

We are getting so close to published! I just got done going through the hard copy book proof for my book, and edits were made. It will now be just 72 short hours or less before my book is live at www.amazon.com and www.crossroadspublishingllc.com. Thank you all so much for walking this journey with me.

Book Live on Amazon –

ANNOUNCMENT!

PUBLISHED BOOK!

My book, "Title", has been published and is now live on the Amazon and Crossroads Publishing, LLC websites. This was such a wonderful journey. Thank you all so much for your encouragement and support through it. Please make sure to post those reviews once you read it.

(amazon book link)

Social Media Posting Examples

Asking for Book Reviews –

Hello, friends! I am taking a moment today to kindly ask you for your time if you have read my book(s). If you could post a review either on Amazon or send one on the Crossroads Publishing, LLC website on the Book Review page, that would be a tremendous help in marketing purposes. Thank you in advance for any time spent.

(amazon book link)

(link to Book Review page on Crossroads website, if you need help with this, let Tonya know)

(attached book review request ad to post, Tonya can make one for you)

Upcoming Book Signing Event-

I have to tell you about an exciting event just around the corner. I will be allowed to have a Book Signing Event at:

Date
Place
Time

I will have books there available for purchase and signing. If you have purchased my book and would like it signed, please feel free to bring it. I would love to see you either way!

Thank you, Crossroads Publishing, LLC and (name of place for book signing event).

If you visit (place name), please thank them for allowing book signing events at their business.

(facebook page or website to place event held, advertisement for them)

Please find my book here:

(amazon book link)

(attach book signing event ad to post (Tonya can create one for you), cover of book, your author picture, etc.)

Marketing Mel says:

Share only what you want to on social media posts. Your posts do not have to look like everyone else's. It is not a competition to see who has the best.

Author Facebook Page

A Facebook Author Page is one of the easiest ways to get information out there about your book. At this time, it is a totally free option. There are some things you can do that would cost a minimal fee, however, overall, it is a matter of post and share… a lot!

Step 1:

The first thing to do in creating an Author Facebook Page is to open your Facebook account. Everything you do on Facebook starts on your personal page. If you do not have a personal Facebook account, one will need to be created for this option.

As shown in the example, look along the options for Pages. Click on that option.

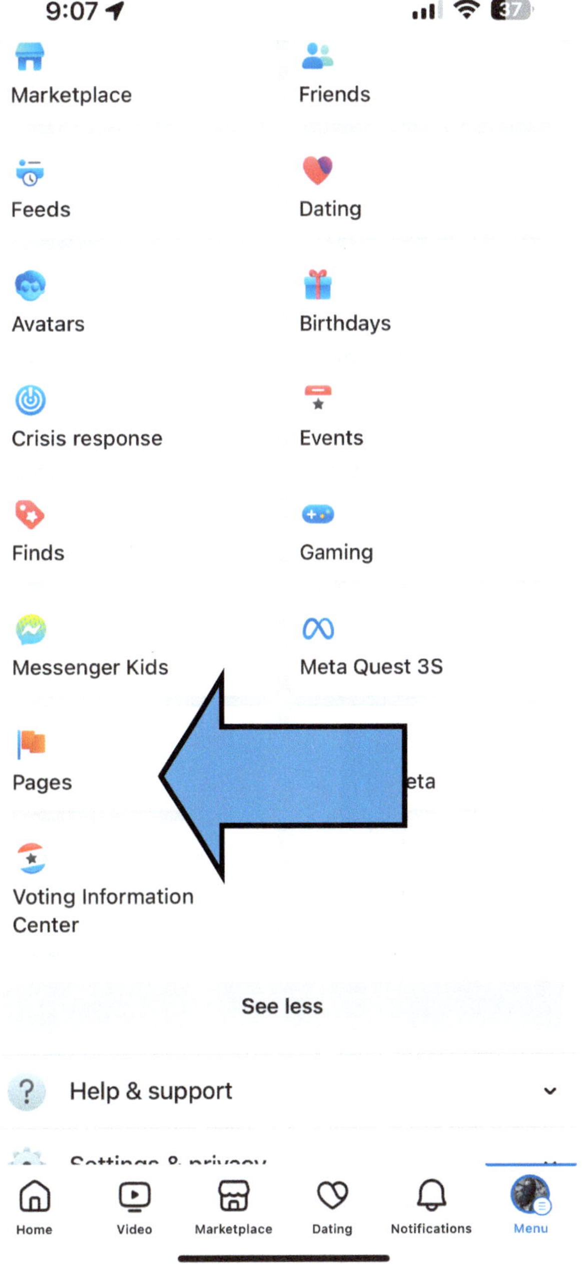

All pictures snipped from Facebook.

Step 2:

On the screen that comes up after clicking on Pages, there will be an option at the top to Create Page. It is shown below. Click on that option.

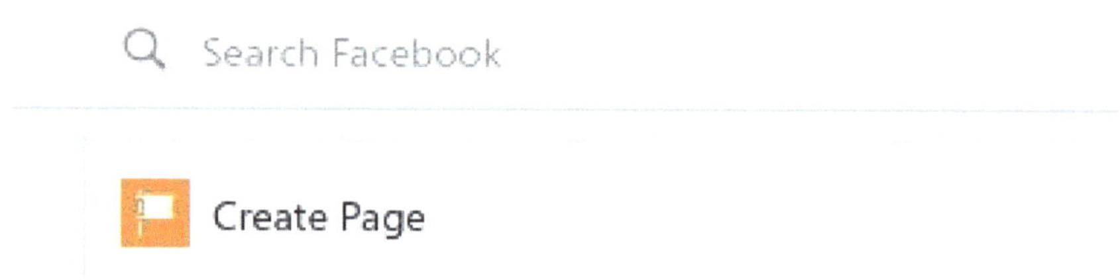

Step 3:

This is the screen that will come up next. Click on Get Started after looking the page over and you realize you are agreeing to continue setting up a Page on Facebook.

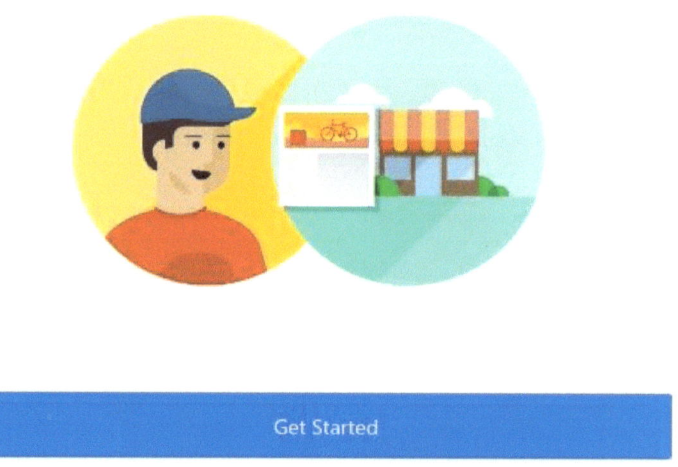

All pictures snipped from Facebook.

Step 4:

On the screen that comes up after clicking on Pages, there will be an option at the top to Create Page. It is shown below. Click on that option. Click Next when you are ready to move forward.

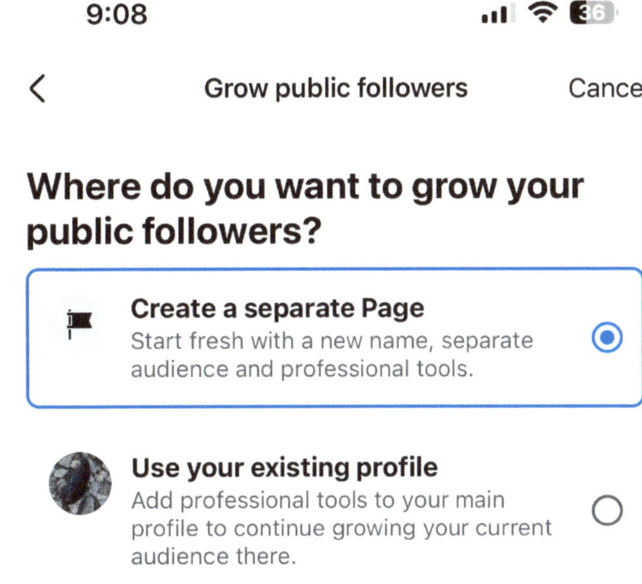

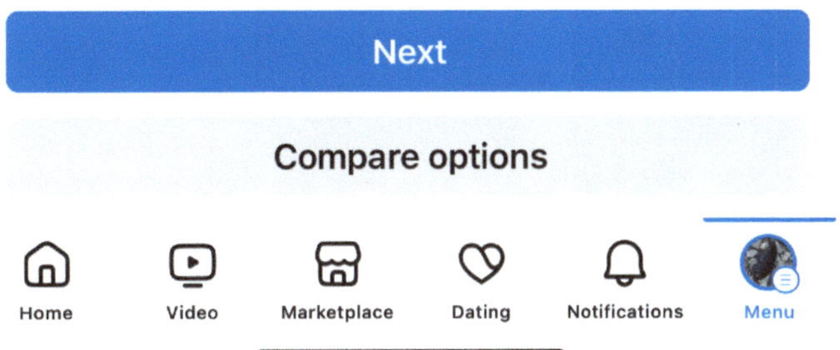

All pictures snipped from Facebook.

Step 5:

While all of the choices in creating a Facebook Page are important, the title of the page might weigh quite a bit in allowing readers to find you. Your page can be titled like a website page with author first, or you can title it something that is important or significant to you. Also, consider making it as short as possible for future marketing endeavors. For example: Author Tonya Andrews. Click Next when completed.

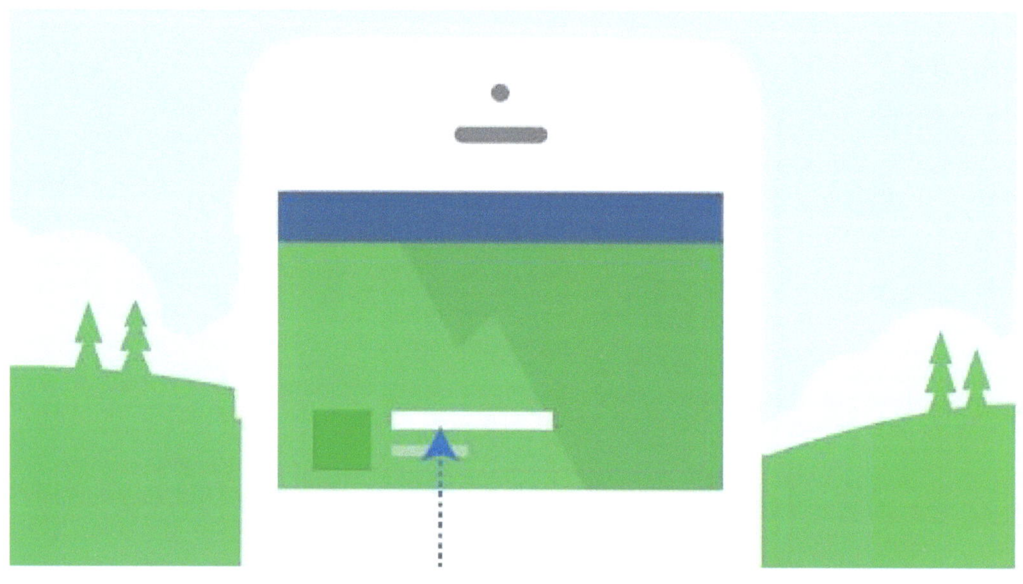

Give your Page a Title

This is how people identify your Page.

Marketing for Authors

The title of your Page should match the name of your brand, business or organization.

Next

All pictures snipped from Facebook.

Step 6:

Choosing a category can prove to be challenging. Use the drop box menu to find the appropriate listing. It will usually bring up another more detailed category after choosing the first one. Click Next when completed.

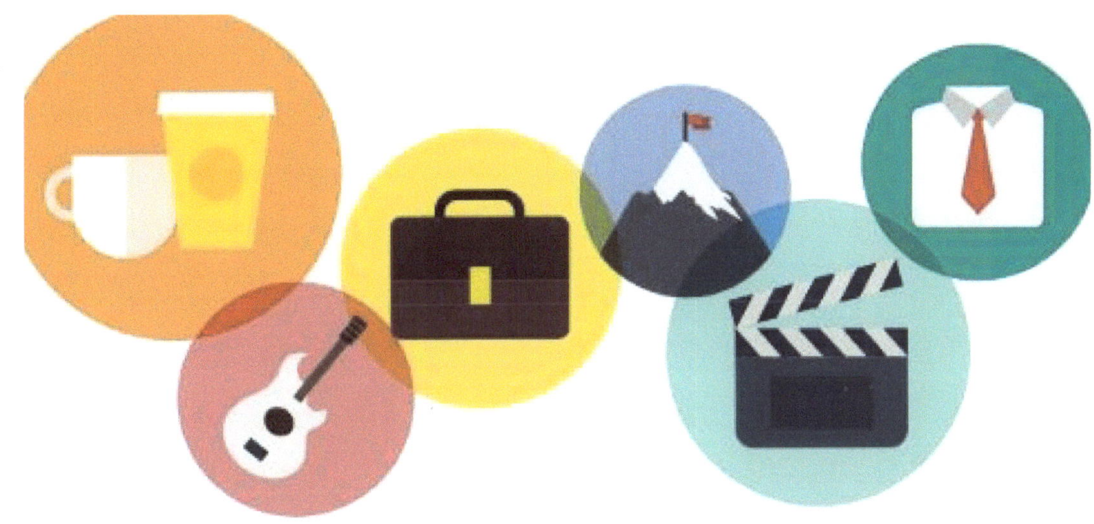

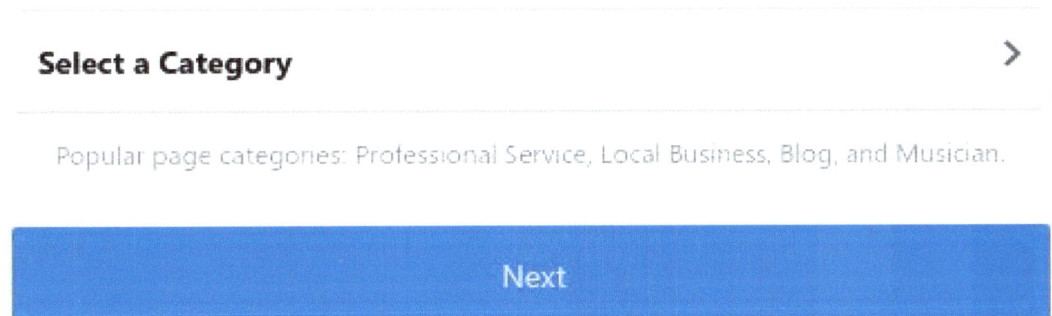

All pictures snipped from Facebook.

Step 7:

This is a very nice option allowed in page creation. If you have your author website already set-up, this would be the place to add it. It can also be added at a later time in a settings menu if needed. If you are not adding it at this time, click skip. Otherwise, type it in the bar provided and click Next.

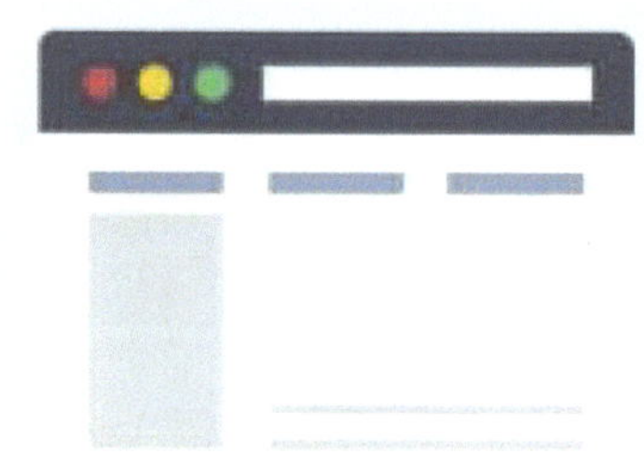

Add your website

If you have a website, add it here so people can get to it from your Page.

http://

You can skip this step if you don't have a website.

Next

All pictures snipped from Facebook.

Step 8:

A catchy profile picture is an important part of creating a page. It can be a picture of you, the author, a picture of one of your book covers or something that is important to you. Please make sure to change the picture every once in a while to keep the interest of your readers. Click Next when the picture is uploaded and what you want.

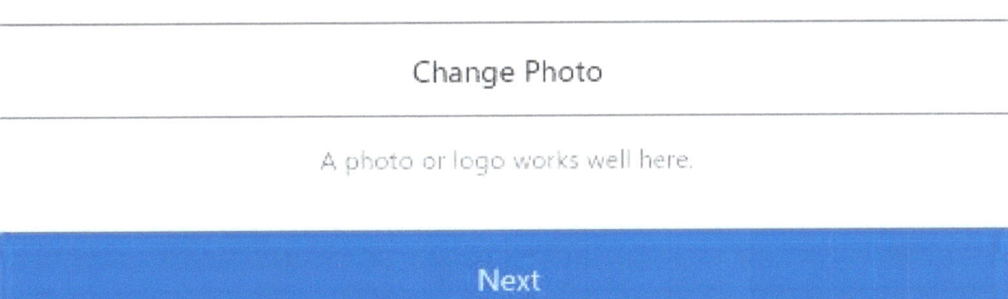

All pictures snipped from Facebook.

Step 9:

A cover photo is not seen as much as a profile picture. It can be used to announce upcoming releases, events or even pictures of books signings. Please also consider changing this photo frequently. Click next when it is complete.

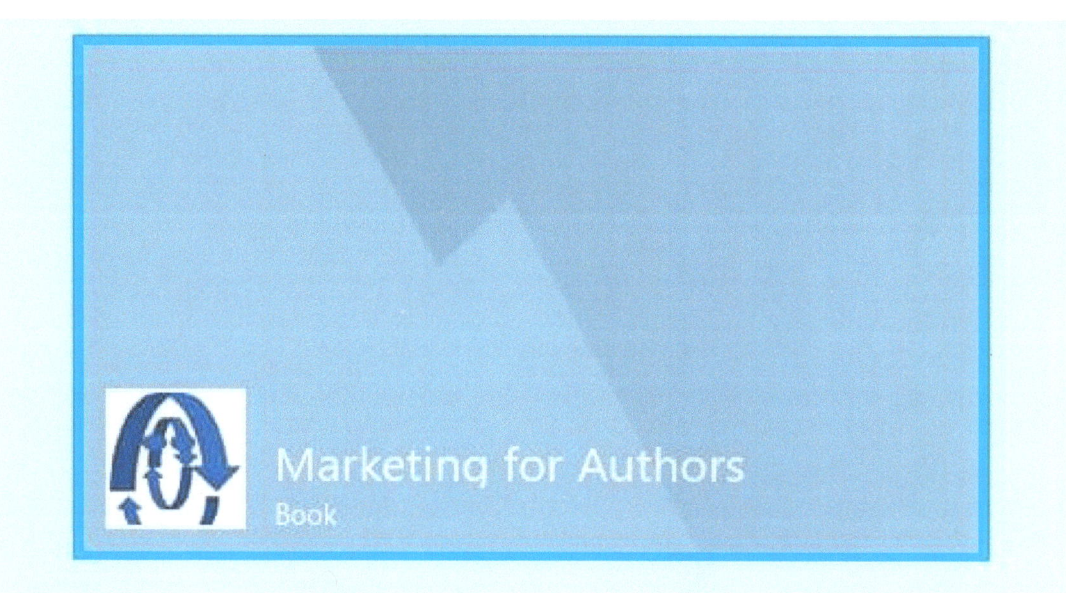

Add a cover photo

Pages with profile and cover photos show up higher in search results.

Upload Photo

Choose a larger, high resolution image for your cover photo

Next

All pictures snipped from Facebook.

Step 10:

Facebook will then create your page with all of the information you provided. There are a few points of interest to immediately consider. The first is to look over your page and make sure all of the information is correct. Most usually, to correct something, a simple click on it will allow that option one way or another.

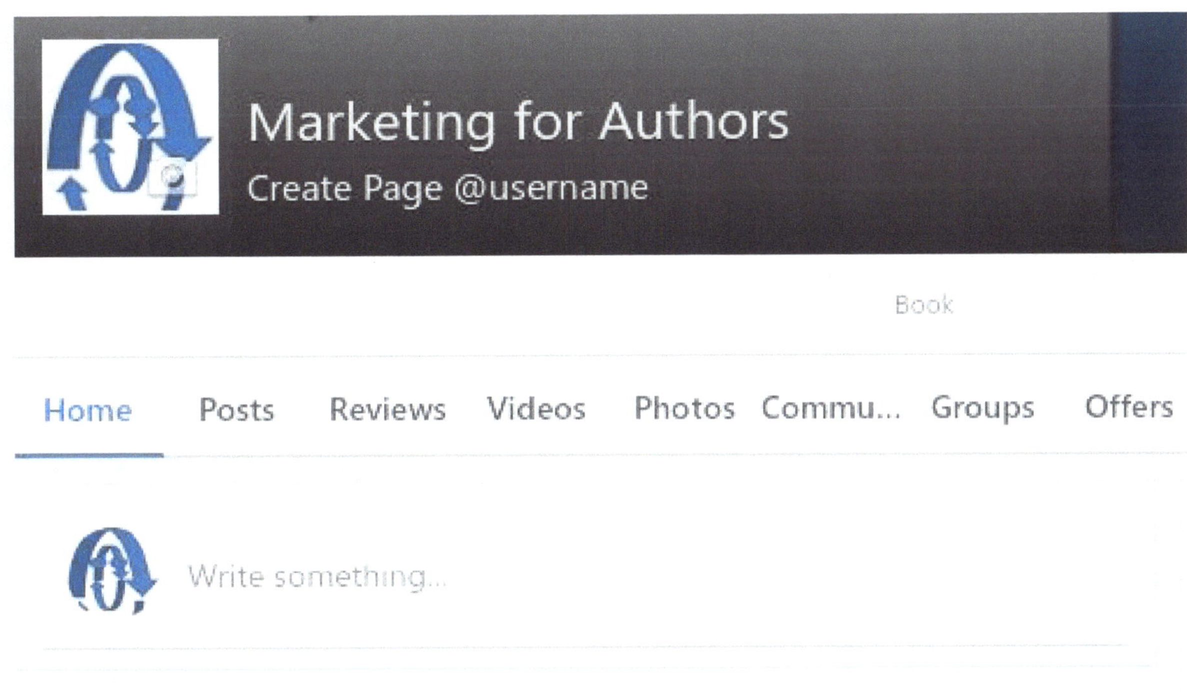

Please Note:

Due to this author's personal Facebook page being hacked, this Marketing for Authors page is no longer monitored. If you would like to contact the author of this book, please email her at ceo@crossroadspublishingllc.com. Thank you.

All pictures snipped from Facebook.

Step 11:

Over to the right on the screen, you will see an option called More. There are two things of immediate interest. The first would be at the bottom to like the page. The next would be Edit Page. This will give you many options for adding several details to your new author page.

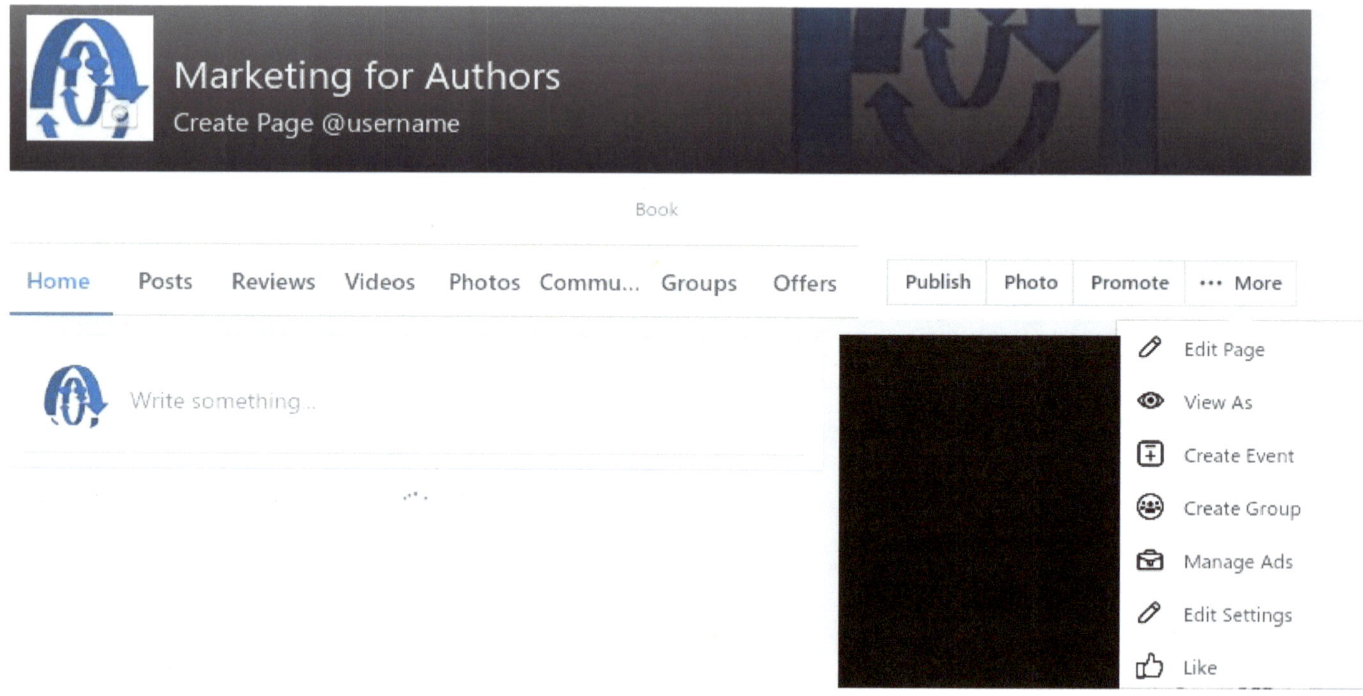

All pictures snipped from Facebook.

Step 12:

These are the Edit Page options. Look through them, and take your time editing and creating. There are many ways to increase your reader views to your page.

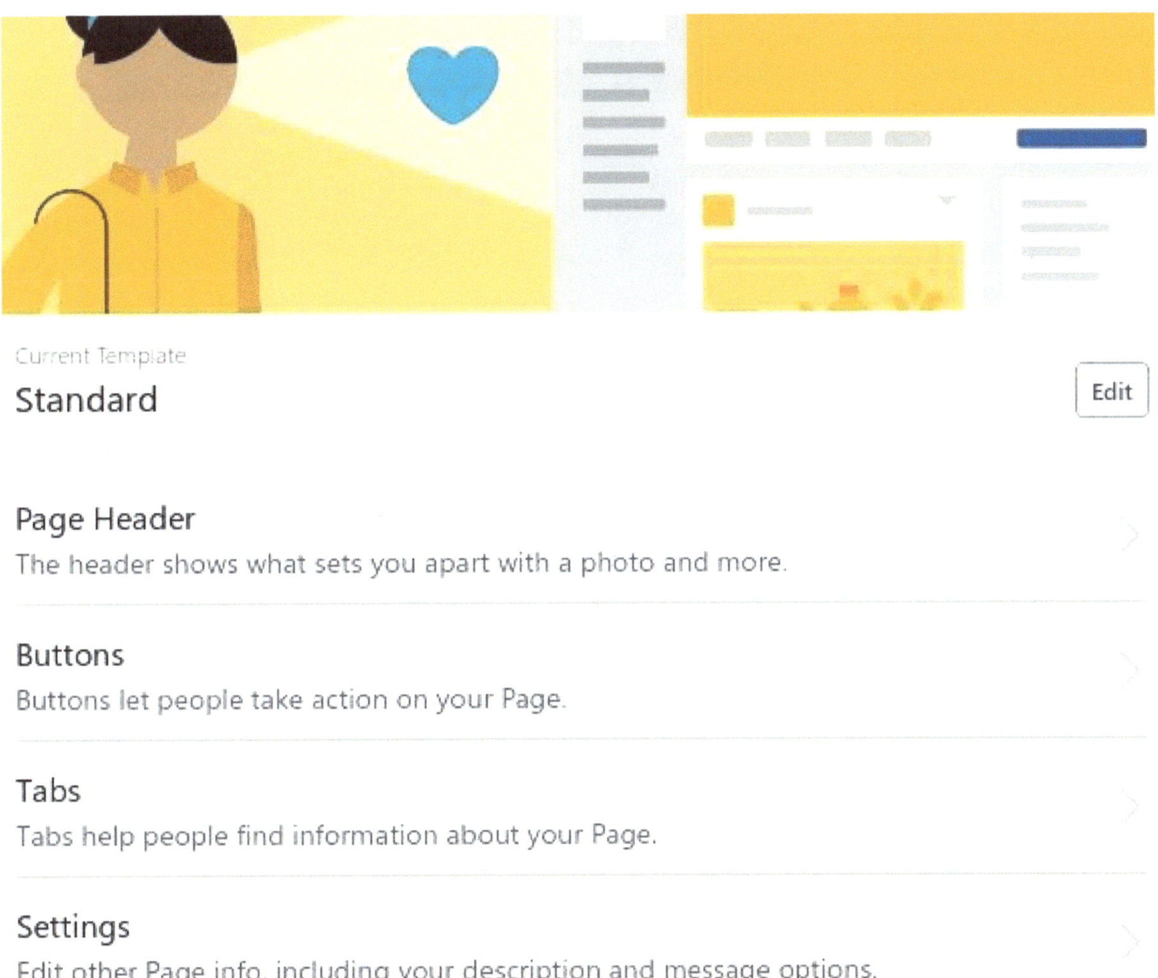

All pictures snipped from Facebook.

Step 13:

Creating your first post. On your main page, find where it says Write something… and click on it (Part 1). It will bring up the options like the second box shown (Part 2). You can type text, add pictures, add places, and go live from your Facebook page. The best way to learn is to just jump in and do it. You can do it!!

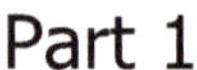

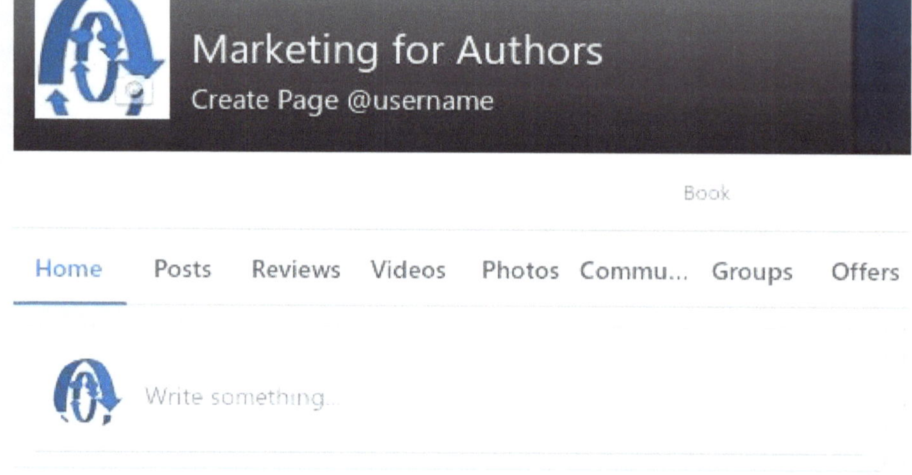

Part 2

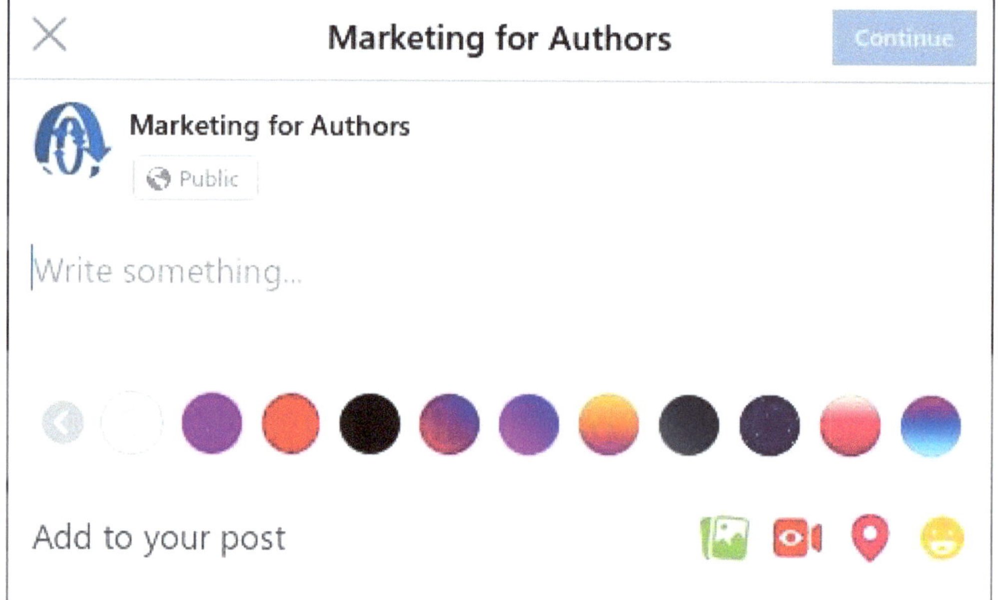

Add a picture to the post

Go Live on your Facebook Author Page

Share your location, for events

Share a feeling or current activity

All pictures snipped from Facebook.

Author Amazon Page

An Amazon Page is one of the most important marketing tools you can have. Once your book is published, it is important to set up your page and "claim" your book right away. These simple steps will lead you through how to set up your page and maintain it.

Step 1: Go to https://author.amazon.com/

Step 2: Click on Join For Free.

amazon author central

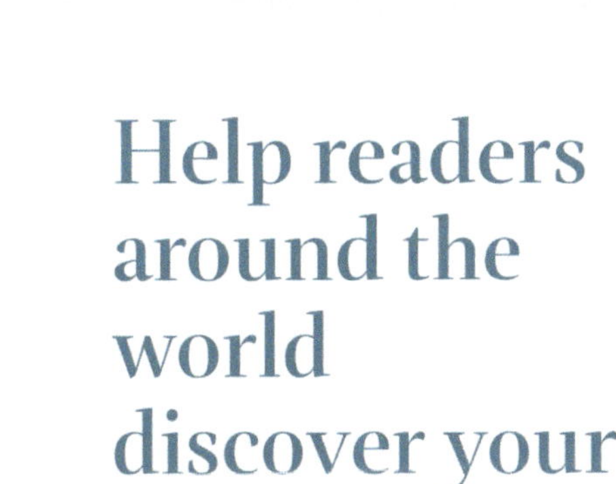

We'll make it easy for you to keep your Amazon Author Pages up to date and stay informed about what's happening with all of your books.

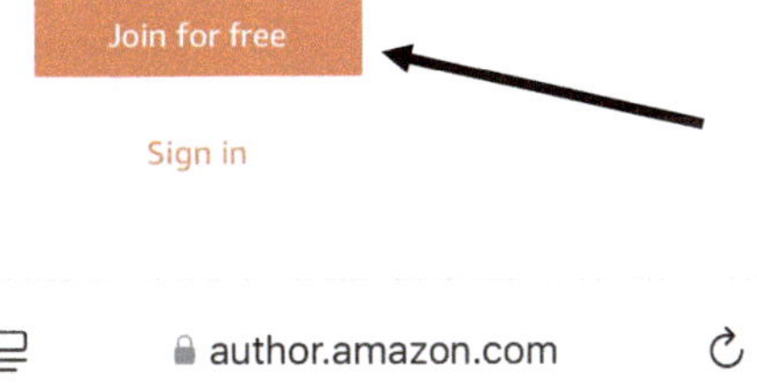

All pictures snipped from Amazon.

Step 3: Fill out the information for a new account. Name, Email, Password, Password Confirm, then push the Create your Amazon account button.

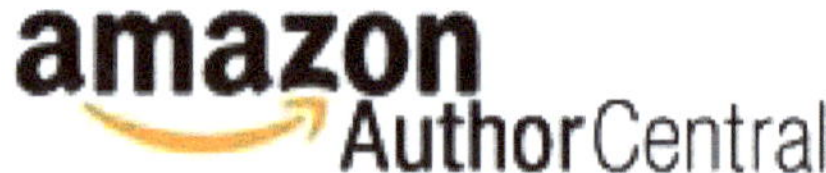

Create account

Your name

Email

Password

At least 6 characters

i Passwords must be at least 6 characters.

Re-enter password

Create your Amazon account

By creating an account, you agree to Amazon's Conditions of Use and Privacy Notice.

Already have an account? Sign-In ▸

All pictures snipped from Amazon.

Step 4: Read and Accept the Author Central Terms and Conditions if you so agree.

Join Author Central: Terms & Conditions

Step 1 of 3

The following terms and conditions outline your use of Author Central. Please review and click the button below to accept.

Updated: May 13, 2009

These Terms of Use are a binding agreement between Amazon Services LLC (with its affiliates, "Amazon" or "we") and you and, if applicable, the author, company or other legal entity you represent (collectively, "you"). Before using Author Central, please read these Terms of Use, all rules, guidelines and policies related to Author Central, including any rules or usage provisions specified on the Amazon.com website, the Amazon.com Privacy Notice and the Amazon.com Conditions of Use (collectively, this "Agreement"). By using Author Central, you agree to be bound by the terms of this Agreement. If you are entering into this Agreement on behalf of an author, a company or another legal entity, you represent that you have the legal authority to bind the author, company or legal entity to this agreement, in which case "you" will mean the party being bound. If you do not have that legal authority, or if you do not agree to be bound by the terms and conditions of this agreement, you may not use Author Central.

1. **General Description of Author Central.** Author Central includes a variety of tools that allow authors to connect with readers through the submission of photographs, images, written communications and other materials (all materials submitted by you through Author Central, the "Submitted Materials") for use on or distribution through sites, services or applications that are owned or operated by Amazon or under any Amazon-owned brand (Author Central and these sites, services and applications collectively, the "Services"). You grant to us a license to use the Submitted Materials on the terms provided below, but you otherwise retain all of your rights in your Submitted Materials. Submission to Author Central does not change your

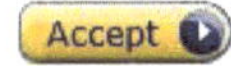

Step 5: Enter your author name and click continue.

Join Author Central: Confirm your identity

Please help us find and identify your books in the Amazon.com catalog.

What is your author name?

My author name is Ann Drews

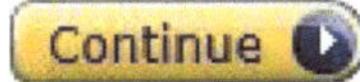

All pictures snipped from Amazon.

Step 6: This next step is very important, however, it is always set-up very easy to use. Enter your author name in the search. Amazon will automatically bring up all of your books. Click "This is my book" by the ones that are yours.

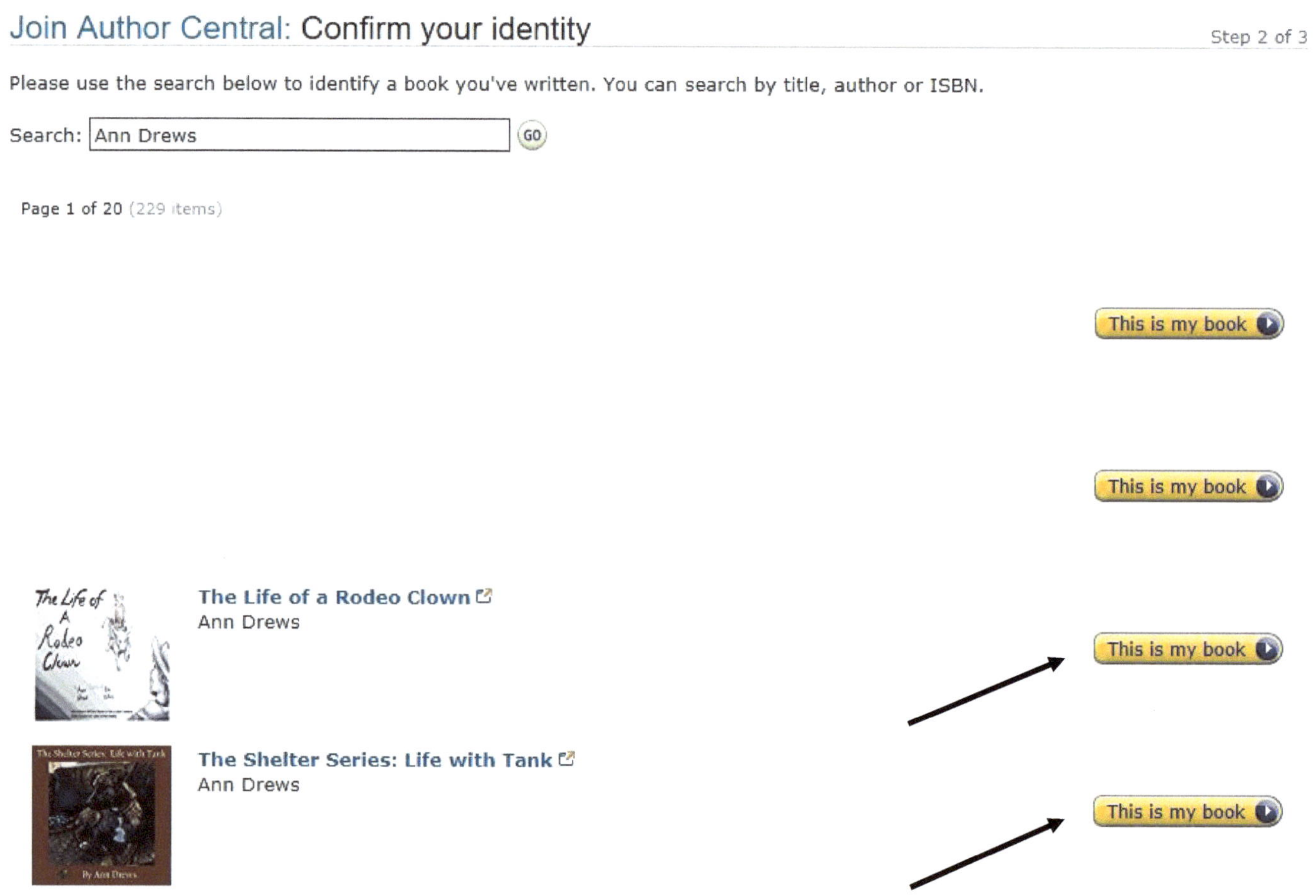

Join Author Central: Confirm your identity

Step 2 of 3

Please use the search below to identify a book you've written. You can search by title, author or ISBN.

Search: Ann Drews GO

Page 1 of 20 (229 items)

This is my book

This is my book

The Life of a Rodeo Clown
Ann Drews

This is my book

The Shelter Series: Life with Tank
Ann Drews

This is my book

All pictures snipped from Amazon.

Step 7: This is what the email will look like for verification processes.

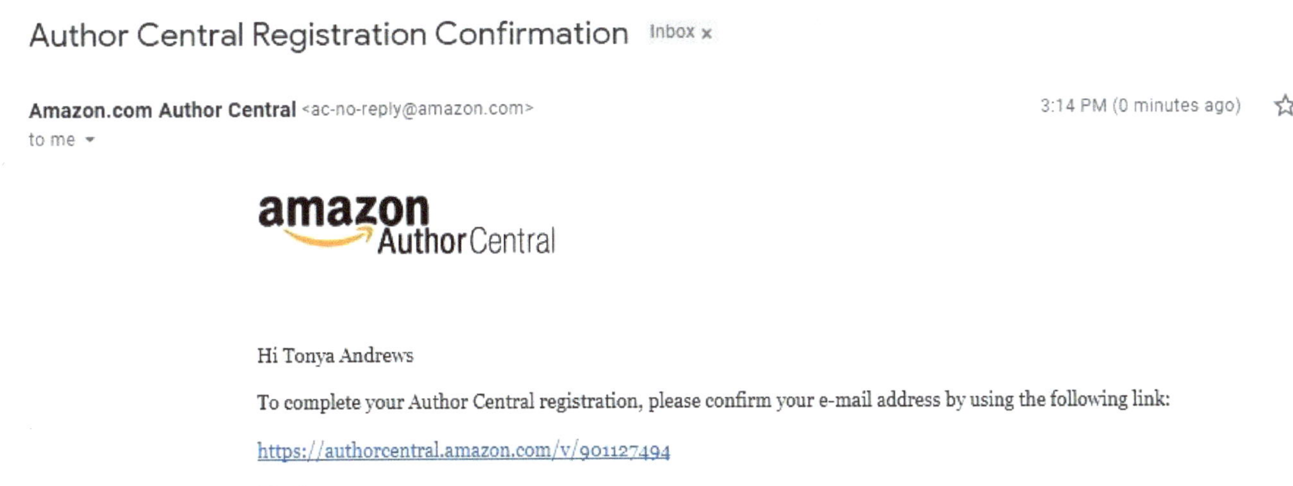

Step 8: Once you verify your email, verifying who you are, you will receive this thank you message. Click Go to Author Central.

Registration Complete

Thanks for confirming your e-mail address!

We have used your account information to verify your identity as Ann Drews. Your Author Central registration is now complete.

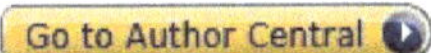

All pictures snipped from Amazon.

Step 9: You have now created your author central account and verified your identity by email. You now have the option to update your author central profile or add your list of books to your profile.

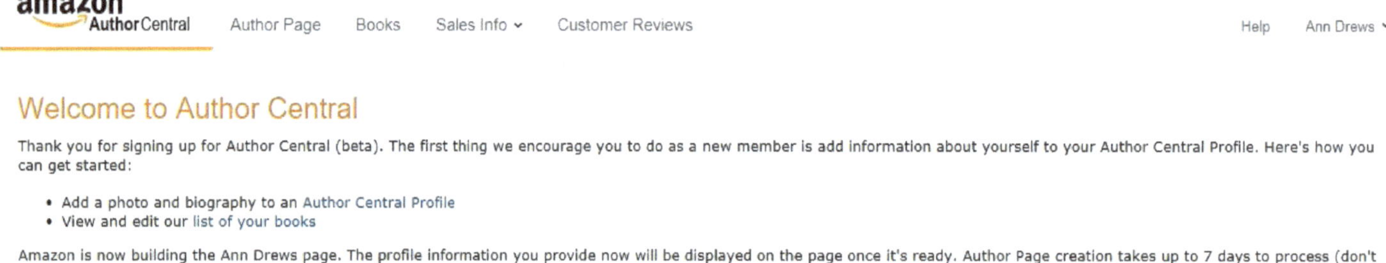

Step 10: If you choose to update your profile first, this is the screen that will come up for you. Follow the directives for each section and update your profile.

Author Page

Author Pages

We are building the Ann Drews Author Page and will e-mail the link to you within 7 days. Content you provide will appear on the Author Page at that time.

Biography — add biography

Tell readers who you are, what you enjoy writing, and more.

Blogs

When the Author Page has finished building, you will be able to display your recent blog posts.

Events

When the Author Page has finished building, you will be able to share speaking engagements, bookstore appearances and other events.

Author Page URL — add link — learn more

Create an easy to share link to your Author Page.

Photos — add photo

Share up to eight photos of yourself.

Videos — add video

Share video interviews, book trailers, or book signing videos.

All pictures snipped from Amazon.

Step 11: The other option is to search for and add your books to your Amazon author central profile list. Clicking on the Add More Books button will allow you to find all of your books for your author profile list.

Books by Ann Drews

These are the books on Amazon's Ann Drews page. Click on any book below to view additional product details or submit corrections.

Are we missing a book?
If a book you've written does not appear in the selection below, you may add it now. Please note that only one edition of each work is shown in this list. Click an edition to make sure all related editions are also listed.

Add more books

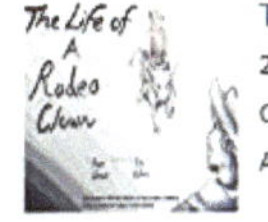

The Life of a Rodeo Clown
2 Editions
Current Sales Rank: #3,643,407 in Books
Average Review: ★★★★★ (1 review)

Add books to your bibliography

close [X]

Search for books you've written by **title**, **author**, or **ISBN** and add them to your bibliography.

Search: willow tree ann drews [GO]

Page 1 of 1 (5 items)

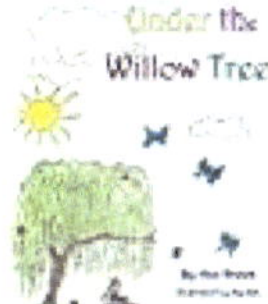

Under the Willow Tree (Volume 1)

This is my book

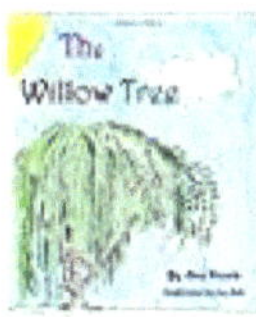

The Willow Tree (The Willow Tree Series)...

This is my book

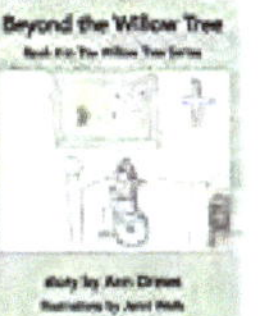

Beyond the Willow Tree (The Willow Tree...

This is my book

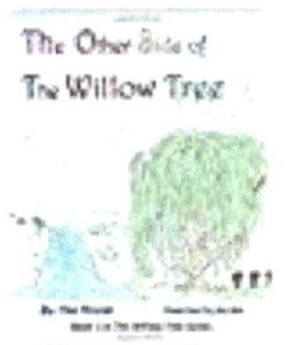

The Other Side of The Willow Tree: Book...

This is my book

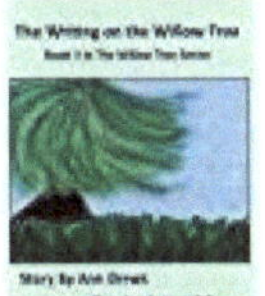

The Writing on the Willow Tree (The...

This is my book

All pictures snipped from Amazon.

You now have an Amazon Author Central Page!

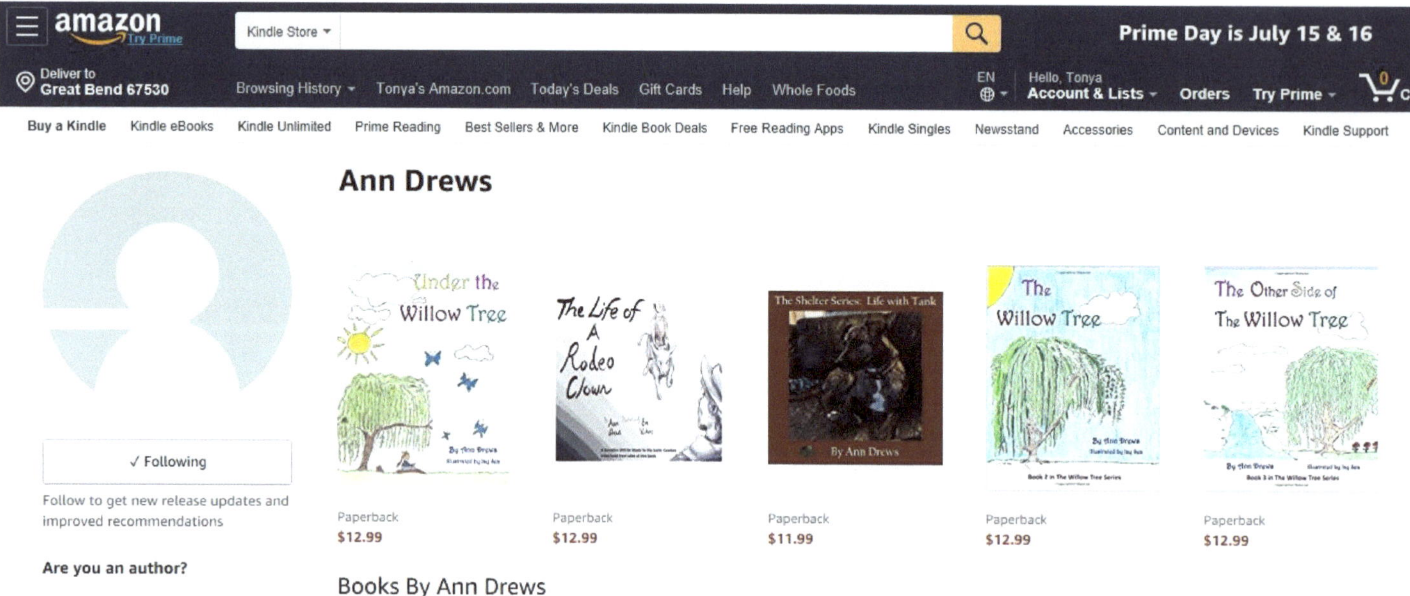

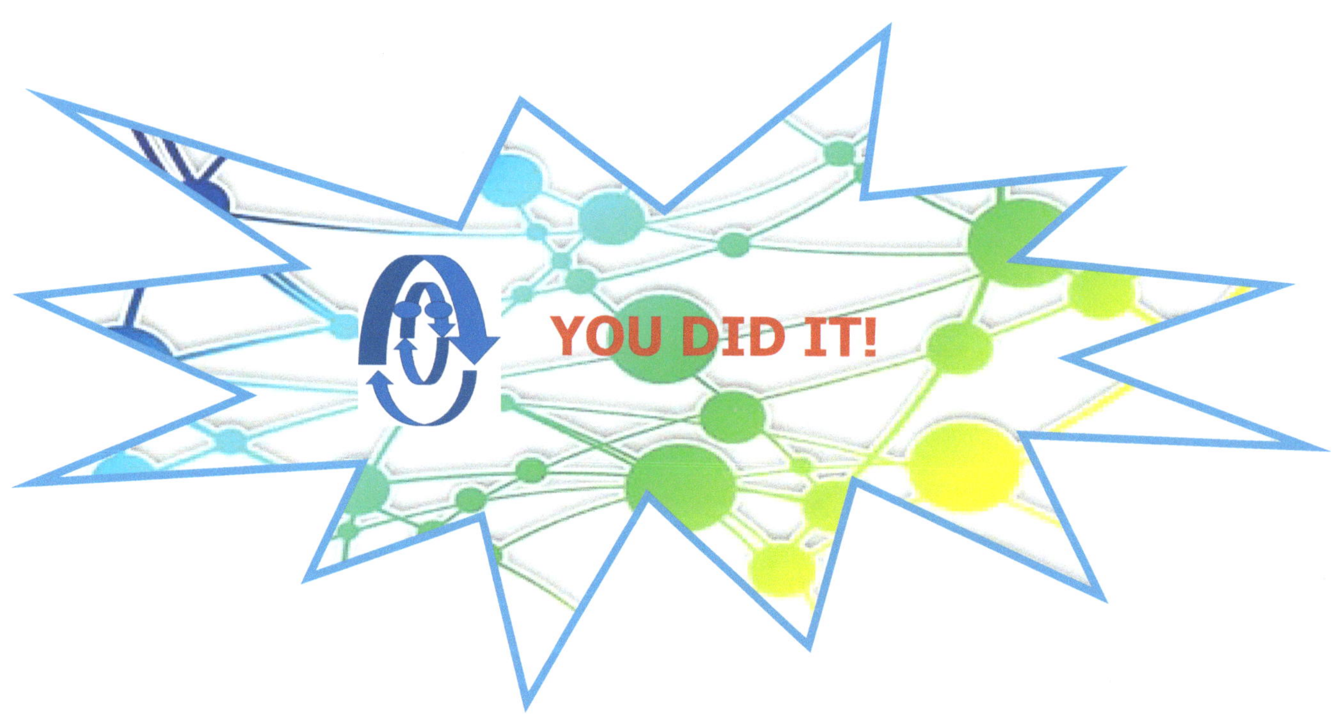

All pictures snipped from Amazon.

In Closing

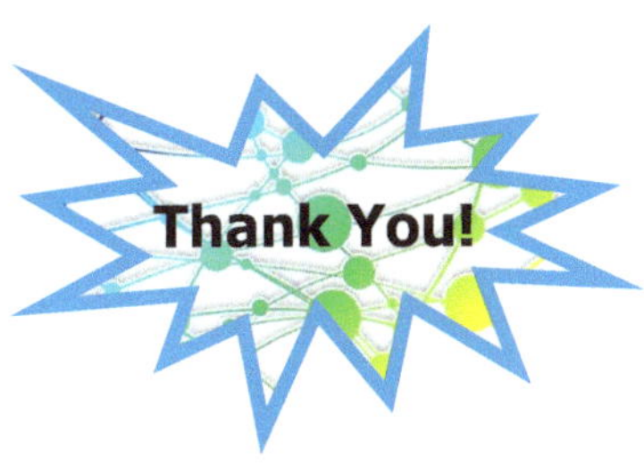

Thank you so much for taking the time to read and look through this book. I am praying you were able to find some helpful tips and ideas for marketing your works. I am available for any questions or comments by email at ceo@crossroadspublishingllc.com.

I have every faith in you that you can do any of this marketing. If there is something that you need help with, please email me. I would be more than happy to assist you or give you some more pointers. I could even explain it in a different way if needed. Having been in marketing for years, I understand these things take time.

Please remember to believe in yourself along this journey. There will be very challenging days, and they will be days you may want to quit. Here are some tips for your author journey in general that may be of some encouragement.

<u>Believe in Yourself</u>

- Make sure you are getting time away by yourself to relax, refresh, contemplate and listen to the guiding for the gift you have been given.
- What are your goals as an author? Are you looking ahead to one year down the road, five years, ten years? Make them attainable and a list to check them off as you go.
- What is your purpose? Are you looking at it from a peaceful side or from a view that keeps dragging you to the past? When you allow yourself time away, and to listen, you find the peace in your purpose.

"The journey to finding our purpose is often such a challenge. We think we know what we want, when we want it and how. However, sometimes, nothing could be further from the truth for our specific purpose. It takes time, experiences, those challenges we so detest and choosing how we will find our way through it all. When we believe in the never-fail, never-ending faith, hope and love gifted to us through sacrifice and service, we realize that our purpose was there all along. We just have to listen to the calling placed on our hearts to move forward walking in that blessed revelation of who we really are meant to be here, and for eternity."

Pastor Tonya Andrews

Thank you again, and have a blessed time writing, marketing and sharing your works.

God's Peace,

Tonya

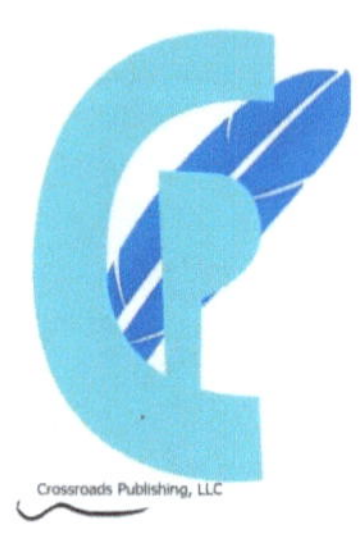

Crossroads Publishing, LLC

An author involved approach to publishing.

For more information, please visit us online at www.crossroadspublishingllc.com.

There you will find:

* Submission Guidelines and Form.
* Company Information.
* Calendar to book an informational meeting with publisher.
* Upcoming Calendar of Events, educational sessions.
* Information on becoming an Illustrator or Editor for Crossroads.
* Recently published books and links to purchase.
* Currently signed information for authors.

For questions or concerns, please contact Owner and CEO, Tonya Andrews at ceo@crossroadspublishingllc.com.

Mention this "Marketing for Authors" book in your book submission email, and receive one cover or illustration at half the normal price.

www.ingramcontent.com/pod-product-compliance
Lightning Source LLC
LaVergne TN
LVHW070219110826
845147LV00003B/604